Sylvia's
Family Soul Food
Cookbook

My beautiful family in our home in Mount Vernon, New York, in 1996.

Sylvia's
Family Soul Food
Cookbook

*From
Hemingway,
South Carolina,
to Harlem*

Sylvia Woods and Family

with Melissa Clark

William Morrow and Company, Inc.
New York

BOOK DESIGN BY RENATO STANISIC

This book is dedicated to our four beautiful children:
Van, Bedelia, Kenneth, and Crizette. May they pass it on to their children and grandchildren
and keep the spirit of Sylvia's alive in everyone's heart for decades to come.
——Sylvia and Herbert Woods

Contents

Acknowledgments

HERBERT AND I HAVE SO MANY PEOPLE to thank—people who gave more than just their time and energy to this project but who gave their love as well.

Many, many heartfelt thanks to:

Terry Frishman, who has been working with our family for so many years that now she's practically a member. We are indebted to her for helping us launch and develop our business on many different fronts, including our line of food products. As she is on any project she works on, Terry was invaluable to us on this one, and I can honestly say that this book wouldn't exist as it is without her leadership and vision.

Our recipe tester, Carol Gelles, who tested and retested every single recipe in the book until they worked perfectly and still retained the spirit of the people who contributed them. Carol likes to say that when she left this project, after spending months cooking soul food favorites, her palate was changed in the best possible way.

Our writer, Melissa Clark, who was able to capture and record the magic of our family stories.

Herbert and me at Bedelia's wedding, 1966.

Doretha Brown-McFadden, who spent hours and hours of her time helping us organize the cookbook and gather the recipes. Her help was essential to this project.

Clarence Cooper and our staff at Sylvia's Restaurant™. Clarence always holds down the fort for us when we're away, and we are very grateful for the hard work done by him and all our employees.

Evelyn Jamison, another member of our extended family, who has been with Sylvia's Restaurant™ for over thirty years. The whole family deeply appreciates all of the sharing and caring she's done through the years.

Mr. and Mrs. Al Finberg for their help in developing our food product line.

Lawrence Jordan, our agent.

All our spiritual leaders—we thank them for their prayers.

Ruth Gully, who was our chef and loyal friend for over twenty years until she passed in 1995. She will always hold a special place in our hearts and we will always miss her kind spirit and wonderful cooking.

And to several people who helped us with this project from the beginning: Frances Donnelly, Gloria Dulan-Wilson, and Sky Williams.

Many thanks need to be extended to all the family and friends who sent us recipes for this cookbook and who attended the cook-off in Hemingway. We really appreciate all the time you took. Although we cannot put everyone's recipe in the book, we are truly very grateful for your efforts. All of you helped us make this cookbook what it is today.

Me at the restaurant, in 1968.

Introduction

IF IT'S TRUE THAT THE WAY TO a man's heart is through his stomach, what can one say about the way to a family's heart? Or the heart of a community or that of a nation? And beyond that, what about the way to the hearts of millions of people all over the world?

Well, my restaurant, Sylvia's Restaurant™, located in the heart of Harlem, USA, is proof positive that you can spread joy to the hearts of all people if you give them something good to eat and a friendly place to eat in. This has been my calling in life. For over thirty-five years, since I opened Sylvia's Restaurant™ in 1962, I have been serving heart-warming and soul-satisfying food to hundreds of hungry people daily. We have fed every kind of person—our relatives, friends, and neighbors; tourists from all parts of the globe; even celebrities and royalty on occasion. And there's nothing that gives me, and now my whole family, as much happiness as knowing that we are giving each and every one of those people something extra: the gift of love that comes free with every meal.

A Long Line of Cooks

People often ask me what makes our soul food so great and I've realized that it's because I come from a long line of great cooks. In fact, I come from a whole community of great cooks. Hemingway, South Carolina, where my husband, Herbert, and I grew up and have our roots, probably has more great cooks per square inch than you would find in most cooking schools. And we didn't go to school to learn how to cook; we learned from our mothers and grandmothers, aunts, uncles, cousins, and neighbors. They raised us, fed us, and taught us. As kids we all attended the same schools and went to church together. Our folks struggled together, worked in the fields, and shared their scarce earnings with those who were not as fortunate. They stuck close together in that little Hemingway community. They raised their families and tried to instill the values of faith, honesty, and trust. They worked hard to build their homes and their lives.

Throughout the decades, people have always shared what they had, and that includes recipes. In the fields, across the back fence, at special events—picnics, parties, births, deaths, holidays, and weddings, whenever and wherever we came together, we brought our favorite dishes, recipes both new and old. And wherever there was food, there were cooks talking about how they prepared it—always swapping ideas and sharing new techniques. Through generations of these exchanges, we found ways of making the food we ate taste even more delicious, go farther, and look better. In doing so we unknowingly created a legacy.

Me and my cousins Tennie and Modestine at the cook-off.

Kenneth at the cook-off.

So what do you do when you come from such a heritage? Especially when such a rich heritage has been what has sustained you through hardships and jubilation, and has been a blessing to many who have never even set foot in Hemingway, much less heard of it?

You write a cookbook. Well, at least that's what my friends and family told me I should do. I would gather together recipes from Hemingway, write them down on paper, and be able to pass them on, not only to our children, grand-children, and great-grandchildren, but to families all over the country whom we've never even met.

But then came the hard part. If you come from a whole community of great cooks, how do you choose which recipes to include?

Well, to narrow it down, we decided to hold a cook-off. We invited our friends and relatives to come to Jeremiah Church on March 29, 1998, to share their favorite dishes. We chose Jeremiah because, as Hemingway's church, it is the cor-nerstone of our community. It's the church where I grew up. It was my mother's and grandmother's church. It's where I still get my strength and support.

When we told the folks at Jeremiah we wanted to hold a cook-off, they responded immediately by spreading the word. Recipes came pouring in from everywhere. Some were handwritten, some typed, some on computer printouts, some E-mailed. Even our minister, Reverend James, and his wife contributed a fabulous recipe for punchbowl cake along with their energy and time.

Then, on a warm day in March, everyone converged on Jeremiah Church. They came from all over, not just to share a recipe or two, but to share their spirit and love for one another and to bond over our common past. When all of our family and friends come together in Hemingway, it's as if we never left. We share our memo-ries, our strength, and our love. This time we shared our recipes.

People brought platters and bowls and pots of amazing food. Tom Cooper made a thirty-gallon vat of his famous lemonade. And we ate and drank and ate some more—helping ourselves to a nibble of chicken, a taste of macaroni and cheese, a bite of greens, a forkful of cake, until we tried every last mouthwatering dish.

But still, choosing what to include in our cookbook was no easy task. We wanted to collect recipes for dishes that I ate when I was a girl, and those newer ones that my children and grandchildren grew up with. We wanted innovative recipes given to us by creative cooks, and traditional recipes that harken back to when our grandparents still prepared their meals on wood-fueled stoves. This book is the result of not just one day at the cook-off but of generations of wonderful cooking. It is not just the product of the people whose recipes we included but the culmination of *all* of Hemingway's talented cooks, who year after year brighten our festivities and get-togethers with the fabulous dishes they prepare, dishes cooked straight from the heart.

And that brings me to one very important point about this book. While all the recipes collected here may seem different, they have one very important ingredient in common. This one ingredient has never been bottled, but it is easily obtained. If it weren't so evident you could almost call it Hemingway's secret ingredient. But it's no secret, really, because many people all over the world use it too, and have been serving it to their families for generations. It's a spice called LOVE, and it is absolutely essential in everything you fix. It's the love that I brought with me to New York City. It's how I was raised. So along with the seasonings I stir in love, and that's what makes every meal I prepare at home or at the restaurant delicious and memorable. And, as everybody knows: Soul food and love are one and the same.

My mother, Julia Pressley, in front of Jeremiah Church.

Throughout the Generations

If you might have been wondering how a young girl could go from picking beans in the fields in a small town in the South to opening one of Harlem's oldest and most respected soul food restaurants with a branch in Atlanta, I can tell you that it was no easy road. My family and I worked hard to get where we are today, but none of us ever minded one bit, because we are all used to hard work. I was brought up that way, never letting a moment be idle. It was a way of being that was passed on from my grandmother to my mother, and she in turn passed it on to me.

Let me start from the beginning: I was born February 2, 1926, to my mother, Julia Pressley. My father, Van Pressley, died just three days after I was born. He died as a result of the repeated gassings he received in the trenches of the First World War. My mother, barely recovered from childbirth and overcome with grief, couldn't make his funeral. She was left a single parent. But there was a lot of love in Hemingway. It was love that made the rest of the family rally around my mother after my father died and helped her raise me.

So, like many children of my generation, I was not just raised by my mother. I was raised by my grandmother as well and by that whole Hemingway community. Knowing that I would be properly taken care of made it easier for my mother to decide, in 1929 when I was three years old, to temporarily leave South Carolina and move to the Brownsville section of Brooklyn, New York, to become a laundress. She left Hemingway because she knew that in order for her to meet her ambition—which at that time was for her to build a little house next to my grandmother's house—she would have to earn more money than she could there. She had a relative who lived in Brooklyn, and after hearing accounts of all the money anyone willing to work hard could make, off she went, leaving me in the loving care of my grandmother.

My mother (seated) *and her cousin Sylvia Hanna.*

My mother and my aunt Sarah in front of my mother's car, about 1959.

Aunt Sarah and Uncle Buddy Burgess, about 1967.

This wasn't at all unusual for the time and place. In fact, there were several children living with my grandmother, my cousins, and other relatives. In Hemingway, it was not unusual for families to help raise each other's children in times of need, and even for families to take in orphaned children. My mother adopted my sister, Louise, when she was about twelve years old and I was about ten. Louise was my mother's cousin, and when her mother got sick, she asked my mother to take Louise in. Herbert and his brother and sister were adopted by his stepfather, who loved them like they were his own, even after his mother's death. We didn't know anything about children being abandoned, raised in orphanages, or left unattended. It was totally out of the question. Regardless of how big a family was, they always made room for one more.

Anyway, Mama (which, until the day she died, I pronounced as "Malma") came to New York in 1929 and worked in a laundry. There she scrimped and

My sister Louise (left) *and friends.*

saved every penny that she earned, placing the money in a homemade satchel attached to a waistband that she wore under her dress at all times. That was her bank. Mama was very frugal; she could squeeze a dollar until the eagle bled.

My mother had a good technique for saving money, and it's a technique that I used when I was saving my money later in my own life. No matter how much money she made, she always changed the singles into large bills, and those large bills were for saving. So if she made eight dollars, a five-dollar bill was folded into her money belt, and the singles and quarters and other change were for spending on rent, food, and other necessities. After a few fives accumulated, those were changed into tens and twenties and eventually into fifties. This is how when I was saving as a young married lady, I was able to stash away a thousand dollars while Herbert was in the navy during World War II. And it was how my mother raised the money to buy the property that was for sale right next door to my grandmother's farm. Together, Mama and Grandma had about sixty acres.

During those five years that my mother was away working in Brooklyn, she would come home and visit as often as she could. I can remember seeing my mother out in a field next to my grandmother's house. She and Grandma were trying to do some measuring, poking little sticks into the ground, with some strings around them. I asked her what she was doing. "This is where I'm going to build our new house," she told me.

Once she was back for good, she bartered with some neighbors to get the house built. This was the way people did things in Hemingway, trading the skills they had with people who had skills they needed. It was the way my mother was able to raise me, build her house, and work her farm without a husband. She exchanged work. The women did the picking in the fields, the washing, mending, quilting, and cooking. In exchange, the male neighbors and eventually the share-cropper whom my mother got to help her with the farm did the plowing, barn rais-ing, and other heavy chores.

When I was a child, I once asked my mother why she didn't get another hus-band to help her on the farm. My mother smiled at my question and answered me honestly. She showed me the envelope she had just retrieved from the mail-box. It was an official letter from the government and inside was my father's vet-erans' compensation check. Mama said, "Sylvia, this is my 'husband'—this check." Then she started naming different women in our community who had remarried after their veteran husbands died, and how some of those second mar-riages didn't work out, but the women had already lost their government checks.

The little house my mother built in 1933. It was the house that Herbert and I spent our wedding night in and the house that Van was born in. There was a fire in that house several years ago.

Mama said, "So you know such and such a one, you see what happened to them." And I would say, "Oh, okay." That was all right with me. She sacrificed her young life to protect me. To see that I was taken care of. I remember she told me so many times that my father knew he was going to die, and he said to her, "I may not ever live to see the baby born, but promise me you will never spoil her—you will raise her, but don't spoil her." She said that she could not bear for me to have a stepfather. She was afraid that I might be mistreated. And that she would lose her check.

So the checks kept coming throughout my young life. But even having this kind of security was not enough for my mother. She still did extra work. Following in the footsteps of my grandmother, my mother became Hemingway's midwife.

When I think back on it, I realize how hard it must have been for my grand-mother when she was Hemingway's only midwife. My grandmother could not read or write. Now can you imagine a woman that can't read or write, but who could deliver a baby? She was one of the strongest-willed people I know, who managed to raise her family in the face of cruel, cruel adversity. You see, just like my mother, my grandmother was widowed while she was still young, after she had given birth to my mother.

To tell you the truth, my grandfather was hanged. It was 1906. There was a robbery at a little country grocery store near where my grandfather lived. The owner of the store—a white man—was killed. Unfortunately, my grandfather was a close friend of the two men who the police accused of the killing. And even though my grandfather had nothing to do with the robbery (he was at home with his family when the crime took place), because he was a friend, the police figured that he had to have been in on it. So they hanged the three friends. My grandmother was sitting behind the courthouse with my mother nursing from her breast when they took my grandfather out to hang him, just like that.

So my grandmother, who did not have a check from the government to pro-tect her, remarried. My stepgrandfather had a little farm and the family lived there for many years until he died. Then his other relatives tried to put my grandmother off the farm, since even though she was my stepgrandfather's legal wife, she hadn't borne him any children as heirs to the property. But my grandmother wasn't going to be put out of her home by anyone. In order to stay, she had to buy these people off and buy that little farm. And she couldn't even read or write. I don't know how she got the knowledge to borrow that money, but that was exactly what she did to keep her home. She borrowed the money and signed the loan papers by making her mark. So you can see where my mother learned the importance of buying a piece of property and building a house of her own.

After our new house was built, I was a little bit sad because I was afraid I would miss living in my grandmother's house with all my cousins to play with. But since the houses were so close to one another, I visited my grandmother almost every day. And having my own house did make me feel special. I can remember the first time we celebrated my birthday in that little home. I was eight years old and my mother threw me a party. She invited all the teachers from my school to come and have dinner with us. It was a very special day, because teachers didn't usually socialize with children after school was over. But everyone had such respect for my mother and grandmother that they came. And I'm sure that in the end they were glad to have come because my mother was quite a cook. I can't remember exactly what she made, but I can guess there was chicken and rice perlow, fried chicken, stewed butter beans and okra, candied yams, collard greens, and probably a coconut cake or an apple cobbler. It was a beautiful, memorable day.

People respected my mother and grandmother because they were the midwives. But that wasn't the only reason. It was also because everyone could see just how hard they worked to raise their children. I remember that even in the worst weather, when the rain came down so hard that we couldn't work in the fields, my mother made sure our hands were busy. Even if other families were allowed to take a break on rainy days and rest, my mother wouldn't allow it. When it rained, that's when we would take time to do our mending, sewing up the holes in our socks and panties, sewing the buttons on blouses, or piecing together a quilt. You just didn't sit around and do nothing. And if we complained about the work, my mother would say yes, we work hard, but this is how we are

Herbert and I renewed our vows on our fiftieth wedding anniversary in 1994. We were just as proud and happy then as we were when we first got married. We're even happier today, surrounded by our beautiful children: (from left) *Kenneth, Crizette, Bedelia, and Van.*

Herbert's grandparents.

able to own a car and electric lights. I remember feeling very lucky to be able to study by a lamp, thanks to my mother.

Made for Each Other

I suppose that here is as good a place as any to introduce the other most important person in my life aside from my mother. And that is my dear husband, Herbert Woods. Our friends and relatives have often said: "If you want to see love in action, you have only to watch Sylvia and Herbert Woods together. They're love personified. It kind of renews your faith in love, because when you're around them there's an aura that reaches out and blesses everyone in their presence." And I'll be the first one to tell you that they're right. I have loved Herbert ever since I was a little girl.

You can even say that food played a part in my finding and falling in love with Herbert, since our relationship began and grew in the bean fields while we picked string beans. It was the children's chore to pick beans every day after school. All of us gathered in the fields to do our work, but also to talk and laugh with our friends. Herbert and I have always believed that divine intervention caused us to meet in those bean fields. Herbert says that we were meant to be together, and he is always finding signs from God to prove it. For example, there's the fact that my mother and Herbert's mother were born on the same day in the same year—January 1, 1906. And there are others, which Herbert can enumerate once you get him started.

Here's one thing about Herbert: He wasn't born in Hemingway. Herbert was born in Richmond, Virginia, where his mother was from, but he moved away

Herbert's parents, Pearl Mintz Woods and Herbert D. Woods.

Here are (from left) Creola, Inez, Cassy, Dorothy, and Kathleen, Herbert's five beautiful aunts, back in the 1950s.

from there when he was four months old. His mother, Pearl Mintz Woods, was a teacher, and his father, Herbert D. Woods, was an itinerant preacher. I understand that Herbert's grandfather gave his father a bale of cotton every year for him to go to school. And even though in those days a bale of cotton was only worth twenty dollars, it got him through.

When Herbert was little he moved around a lot, following his father from church to church. Herbert had a hard time with this kind of life, since just as he got settled where he was, he'd have to pack up and move, leaving his newly made friends behind. All he ever wanted was to have a place where he could stay for a long, long time. And once he moved to Hemingway, he found that little boy's dream.

Unfortunately, that dream came at a very high price. Herbert's family didn't stop moving until his father died of pneu-

Herbert's sister, Annette Bass, about 1964.

monia when he was thirty-three years old. But his mother, Pearl, managed to take care of the family by teaching and saving. It was a hard life; teachers didn't get paid that much back then, especially black teachers. They were lucky if they got forty dollars a month. Eventually Pearl got transferred to a school in Friendship, South Carolina, which is ten miles away from Hemingway. That's where she met Herbert's stepfather, who was also a minister, Reverend Robert Donnelly. They got married and moved into his house.

Poor Pearl lived only a year after getting married. She was also thirty-three when she died, ten years after Herbert's father. But it was like God had a hand in finding those children a home near me. When Herbert, his brother, and his sister moved into their stepfather's house with his four children, all the kids immediately became sisters and brothers. There was no question when Pearl died that Reverend Donnelly would raise her children, because by then they were like his children, too.

Anyway, it was during the same year that Herbert's mother married his stepfather that Herbert and I met—in 1937. I was eleven and Herbert was twelve. Herbert remembers that day even better than I do, which is hard, since it burned into both our memories as powerfully as can be. He has often said to me, "Sylvia, whenever I see you I still see that girl I met in the bean fields on that wonderful day. You were so beautiful, with your dark chocolate skin and big, soulful eyes. I was smitten with you before we ever spoke and before I even realized how gentle and smart you were."

It was more than sixty years ago, but I remember seeing Herbert for the first time just like it was yesterday. I saw this little boy in that bean field, and I remember Herbert's knees stuck out of his pants and that he was barefoot, same as me. But I swear I couldn't take my eyes off that little brown-skinned man to save my life.

You see, even when I was a little girl I always knew that I wanted to marry and have a large family. I never could draw, really. I couldn't draw a cat or a dog, but I could draw the figures of a woman and a man, a husband and a wife, and little figures of boys and girls, their children. I think it's because I felt lonely without a father. So when I grew up, I'd have a husband and a large family, which I'd draw in picture after picture and save in my room. Pictures of my future family in front of my future house. It was my heart's greatest desire.

My beauty school graduation photo, class of 1942, Brooklyn, New York.
I was so hurt because someone sat in front of me and blocked me out of the picture.
I'm in the second row, second from the right, behind the hat.

So when I met Herbert, all I could think of was, This is the man I'm going to marry. Since we were in the same school, it was easy for us to find little bits of time to be together. At the end of the school year, in May, all the children would get together and put on a play. That year, the teacher let Herbert and me gather the honeysuckle that we used to decorate the stage. Back then, Hemingway was filled with honeysuckle. So whenever I smell honeysuckle, I think of our young love. We dawdled as we gathered the flowers, holding hands. It was the perfect opportunity for us to be together; once school was out, we wouldn't see each other except for church on Sunday.

In our early years, before we were old enough to officially keep company, we had to do most of our visiting in and after school. But we lived in different directions from that little unpainted schoolhouse, so we couldn't walk home together, and Herbert couldn't carry my books. All we could do was look at each other, waving frantically as we walked farther and farther apart. I was always afraid one of us would fall or trip in a hole, since we weren't paying attention to anything except each other.

Then there were all the notes we wrote. Since neither of us had telephones back then, we had to communicate with each other by writing. We wrote notes in the classroom, which the teacher sometimes found. She would say, "Bring that note up here, Herbert. Bring that note up here!" Then Herbert would have to get up there and read my note in front of all the other children. But even that didn't stop us. Then there was the time that Herbert's mother got ahold of one of our notes. I had given it to my brother-in-law Ernest to give to Herbert, and when Pearl figured out what was going on, she wanted to stop it then and there.

"What was that that Ernest gave you?" she demanded of Herbert, all the while knowing it was my note. When Herbert handed it over, she said, "Now you

Herbert in the navy, 1942. I thought he looked so grown-up in his sailor suit!

Herbert and me in Coney Island while Herbert was on leave from the navy in 1944. I was pregnant with Van at the time and felt so sick! But I knew it was the only time Herbert and I would have together before he went back to sea.

tell Sylvia you are gonna go to college. And, if you don't tell her, I'll tell her." Herbert was really upset at the time, but now we laugh when we think about how she tried to break up our little puppy love. What she didn't know was that God had a hand in this, and that you just can't stop the inevitable. I'm very sorry she didn't live, because I know she would have been happy about us. It was just a week or so after the note that she passed away. After Herbert's mother died, it seemed that my mother was always kind of quietly looking out for him, though she never really said anything. Everyone just kind of felt it.

When we would go out to basketball games or picnics with our school, my mother would make a sandwich for me to take on the trip and she would make a sandwich for Herbert. She would say, "Well, Herbert ain't got no mother," and a phrase she would always use was "a motherless child has a hard time." She would make a biscuit with jelly, her homemade jelly, or a sausage patty, and maybe a piece of fruit or a bit of cobbler and pack it up for Herbert. He was so grateful that my mother looked out for him.

Finally, when we were old enough, I guess when I was about fourteen, Herbert was allowed to come over to the house and court me. Courting days were twice a week, on Wednesday and Sunday evenings, from six o'clock until nine. I don't know why it was on Wednesdays, except maybe it was a custom left over from slavery times. Anyway, after washing up from supper I'd go in the bedroom and fill the tin washtub with a pot of boiling water and a bucket of cold water, which was enough to fill the tub with about six inches of water. I'd bathe, brush my hair straight down, and put on my little cotton dress and white socks. Once Herbert got there, we'd sit under the moonlight and talk about how even when we were apart, we were still together because we could both gaze at the same moon. It was very romantic . . . until about five minutes to nine, when my mother would start clearing her throat, indicating that it was time for Herbert to leave and make the three-mile trek home.

That trek was probably the only thing that Herbert didn't like about courting me. The road was dark and scary, since it passed through a swamp and by a cemetery. And the old people would scare you to death! Back then we didn't have television or radio for entertainment, so people would sit around the fire or on the porch and tell stories, ghost stories about that cemetery and the swamp. They'd tell you about men with no heads walking around at night. So when Herbert got to the bridge over the swamp, he'd tiptoe across so quietly that he could barely hear himself, so the ghosts and headless men wouldn't hear him and come to get him.

I thought Herbert and I could just be together forever. But after I finished school, my mother decided that I should move to New York City and learn how to be a beautician. She said that I would have better opportunities in New York. I knew she was right. One minute I was excited about going, but the next minute I was sad. I didn't want to leave Herbert. Mama said I could open my own shop once I finished beauty school, and that I could come back and visit in the meantime.

But poor Herbert was crushed. He had had so much loss in his young life that when he heard I was going away, he thought I'd never come back, even though I promised him that I would. You see, when his father died, and Herbert was a tiny boy, his mother didn't tell him his father had passed. She said he had to go away. He just never came back.

So when I told Herbert that I would surely come back, he said, "You promise?" And I said, "Cross my heart and hope to . . ." I almost said "to die," but I caught myself and said, "Cross my heart, I'll be back."

And then, for the first time, Herbert said to me, "I love you, Sylvia Pressley."

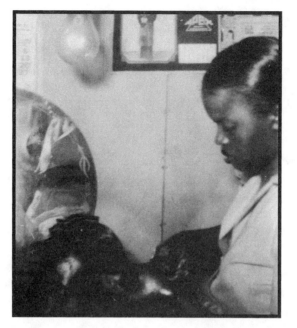

Me, doing hair in the beauty parlor that I built in Hemingway, about 1949. Herbert was away at sea.

Van and Bedelia in Hemingway, about 1951.

And I said, "I'll always love you, Herbert Woods."

But then my mother came out of the house and took me to the train *station*. I missed Herbert even before I got on the train. Beauty school perked me up for a little while. But still, everywhere I turned, everyone I saw reminded me of Herbert. I even walked up to a kid who looked a lot like him, only to find out it was someone else. Those were the hardest days for me, being away from him for so long. On top of that, I kept looking for gold coins in the streets of New York City. I had daydreams about filling my purse with them. And all I saw were drably dressed people. I was so disappointed I guess I started to cry. And my mother asked me what was wrong. I said, "If today is Sunday, why aren't people dressed up?" My mother told me people in New York worked seven days a week. Then I asked her where was all the gold that was supposed to be in the streets. And she just looked at me and hugged me.

Me, in California, about 1949.

In the meantime, Herbert was down in Hemingway missing me as much as I missed him. And that's when he got this idea that if he enlisted in the navy, they would ship him to New York. Herbert's brother, James, whom we also called BB, tried to talk him out of it, but he wouldn't listen. But when he went to the recruiting officer and tried to enlist, Herbert was told that he was too young. He left, all the while still trying to figure out a way to enlist. So Herbert figured out the schedule of the recruiting officer who had rejected him. And when that officer took his lunch break, Herbert walked in dressed in his best Sunday suit and enlisted with the other officer on duty, who didn't know him. Herbert was sworn in real fast before that first officer came back. Herbert shook the enlisting officer's hand, said, "Thank you, sir," and rushed out.

Me and Bedelia, about 1962.

When Herbert told his stepfather, Reverend Donnelly was sad. But he said, "Well, there ain't nothing I can do about it. You're a man now." Herbert told me that he kept picturing himself on a big boat heading for New York Harbor. Instead, he ended up in San Francisco, passing under the Golden Gate Bridge. He was assigned to kitchen duty, making dozens of biscuits for the officers.

And there I was in New York, thinking I would never, ever, see my Herbie again. I kept saying to my mother, "What if he don't come back?" And she would say, "Sylvia, that boy done been through too much, he's got too much living left to do. He went through too much trouble to get to you for him not to do it. God's not going to let him die now. He'll be back."

But that took two long, hard, lonely years and a lot of letters. It just looked as if we were never going to be in the same place at the same time ever again. Eventually, though, we were. When Herbert walked off that train in New York, I hugged him so hard I almost knocked him over. He looked so handsome and grown-up in his sailor suit. We couldn't take our eyes off each other, just like in the bean fields, and we sat giggling and talking over chocolate shakes at the drugstore near my room.

Herbert always said that on that reunion day, he couldn't bear to look away from me because he was afraid that if he blinked or turned his head, I would disappear, vanish before his eyes. He held my hand with one of his, and then reached inside his pocket with his other hand. Then he opened my hand and placed a ring inside it, kissing my fingers as they closed around the band. I had never been so happy in all my life. I slipped the ring on my finger, placed my hand over my heart, and said, "I'm going to wear this ring forever."

And we got married just as soon as the license came. I had on a green dress I'd been saving for a long time, and Herbert had on his uniform. After we were married we couldn't stop kissing each other. Even when the minister tried to break us up, we just kept right on kissing. That was January 18, 1944.

And we still haven't stopped kissing, even after fifty-five years of marriage.

From Hemingway to Harlem

Marrying Herbert Woods was certainly the best thing I had done to date in my young life. I was eighteen years old and he was nineteen. At the time, we knew that life lay open ahead of us, and we could make it into anything we wanted if we worked hard enough. But we didn't really have a grand plan. And we certainly didn't have any idea that one day we would be restaurateurs.

Me, in the old restaurant, in 1968. We moved two doors down the block later that year.

No, life went on pretty much as it had been. I finished beauty school and went home to Hemingway to build a beauty parlor on my mother's farm, and Herbert went back to the navy to finish out his term. By this time, I was pregnant with our first child, Van.

While we were building the beauty parlor, which originally was meant to be one or two rooms, my mother suggested that we make it bigger, to include some living space for Herbert and me once he came home for good. So we built a three-room house, with the beauty parlor in one big room in the front and a bedroom and kitchen in the back. The house was very modern by Hemingway standards; it even had running water, which I needed to do hair. It was the first place I'd lived in Hemingway that had running water. While Herbert was still at sea, my mother decided that it was time for her to give up working on the farm, so she gave her little house and land over to our relatives to farm and moved in with me.

Members of my sewing club, about 1970. Each one of us made the outfit that we are wearing in the photo. That's me, fourth from the right.

I did pretty well for myself in that beauty parlor. I charged $1.50 a person and saved my money in a satchel around my waist like my grandmother taught me to do. In fact, I believe that it was my grandmother who made me that satchel, out of yellow horse print, which is the same, strong, stretchy material that they use to make Ace bandages. Anyway, I saved so well that when Herbert got back, not only had I completely paid for the beauty parlor but I was able to show him over a thousand dollars in cash.

I was also able to show Herbert our brand-new son, whom my grandmother had helped deliver into this world. We were very proud.

Well, we made a plan to move to New York. It just seemed like there would be more opportunity in a big city than in our small Hemingway community. We had some relatives living in Harlem on 131st Street, so Herbert and I packed up and moved north, taking our baby, Van, with us.

Those first few years in New York just seemed to float by. I was a full-time housewife, taking care of Van and keeping the apartment, which was five large rooms, clean and cozy. Herbert got a job at a dye factory in New Jersey, but eventually he decided that it would be best to do a second term in the navy. This time, he went to cooking school to learn how to bake, so he could get a better, more skilled job in a ship's kitchen. Off he went to California and off I went back to Hemingway for a little while, but then I ended up back in New York, where I gave birth, in 1948, to our first daughter, Bedelia.

This back-and-forth from Hemingway to New York set the tone for the rest of my life. I never really felt like I lived in one place or the other. I lived in both places and they seemed to come together for us, making the trip from South to North part of the fabric of our lives. Sometimes it seemed as if Hemingway was a suburb of New York, or that New York was the big city down the road from Hemingway. It was a seamless flow rather than a series of moves.

When Bedelia was a few months old and Herbert was still in baking school in the navy, I decided that the best thing I could do was to move to California to be near him. I missed him terribly, but also I wanted to see if I thought Herbert and I could make California our new home. I left the children with my mother in Hemingway while I checked it out, and took the train out west. It took Herbert and me seven months to realize that we belonged in the East. We moved back to New York in 1950 and didn't really leave again except to go to Hemingway.

My sister-in-law had kept the apartment on 131st Street for us, so we could return without the stress of finding a new place to live. Once we got settled, we brought the children back to live with us, and Herbert worked as a taxi driver. The money was okay, but it wasn't what I wanted for my family. I am just like my mother in so many ways, and one is that I always have to keep busy, working hard to better our lives. So I started fixing hair in that apartment. But while I had a few loyal clients, the money wasn't as steady as a regular job, and it was harder for me to make plans without being sure where the next dollar was coming from. I knew that I needed to find a job, so I took off my housewife's apron and found myself employment in a hat factory in Queens.

In a few years, I was pregnant again, this time with Kenneth. As with Bedelia, when the time came for me to give birth, two maternity nurses came over and helped me deliver my child in the bedroom of our apartment. Back then, most women gave birth at the hospital, like I did when I gave birth to Crizette over a decade later. But I am jumping ahead of myself here.

For as long as we had that apartment in New York, we also had a constant stream of visitors from the South, our cousins and friends and other relatives who left their farms to come to the city in search of opportunity. Many a Hemingway mother felt better about letting their grown-up children come to New York knowing the kids could stay safely with Herbert and me. My aunt Sarah (and uncle Bucky) sent all five of their children to stay with us before each one eventually left to live in Connecticut. And our door was always open, even if some people had to lay their heads on the floor. Our apartment was a way station for these relatives, who stayed just long enough for them to get on their feet, find a job and an apartment, or get married. Three young ladies got married out of that apartment. Those were good times; I love to have my family around me.

When Kenneth was still a small baby, in 1953, Herbert and I decided to send him, Van, and Bedelia down south to live with my mother. I had hired a baby-sitter to look after the children, but I didn't think she was doing a very good job and I worried that my children weren't being properly looked after. Then Kenneth developed a terrible case of diaper rash and my suspicions were confirmed. I fired that baby-sitter and sent the children to my mother, who would bring them up in the country and teach them what she had taught me: strength, faith, and self-sufficiency. These were important lessons to learn, and I knew that my mother would care for and love these babies just as I did myself.

In a way, I was following in my mother's footsteps. When she was a young lady and I was a young child, she left me with her mother and went to work in the city to save the money to buy her house. I was doing the same kind of thing, although at the time I didn't know that, in fact, we weren't going to be buying a house very soon—we'd be buying a restaurant.

Of course, if you told that to me then, I would have laughed. I had rarely ever eaten in a restaurant, let alone worked in one. If it hadn't been for my cousin

Coute, I doubt I ever would have thought of becoming a waitress. But Coute had a waitressing job at a little luncheonette on Lenox Avenue and 126th Street, just a few blocks from my apartment. She was about to leave her job and she convinced me to go in and ask Mr. Johnson, the owner, if I could have it. And I knew she was right. You see, even though I didn't mind factory work, I thought I could save more money at Johnson's. First of all, I wouldn't have to spend money on carfare, since the restaurant was only a five-minute walk from my home. Second, in a factory job, I had to have several dresses in good shape, one to wear each day of the week. If I worked for Johnson, I'd wear a uniform, and could save my street clothes. And I also wouldn't have to worry about bringing lunch, which I made every morning, just like my mother did when she worked as a laundress.

Really, there was only one little problem and that was my inexperience. But I gathered up all my nerve and marched into Johnson's luncheonette back in 1954. I introduced myself to Mr. Johnson as Coute's cousin, and when I asked for that job, I looked him dead in his eyes. I can remember that; I was scared to death. I told him that I had worked in a restaurant in Hemingway, South Carolina. Johnson, who was from Charleston, South Carolina, knew that I was lying, since the only restaurant in Hemingway was segregated. But he gave me the job anyway. I worked there for eight years, saving my wages and most of my tips. Saving for . . . I didn't even know what. But I saved and saved nonetheless.

Now Johnson owned three restaurants, and there reached a point when he couldn't continue to run them all. So he chose to sell this one, even though it was just a small mom-and-pop operation, with one long counter and a few booths against the wall. So one day Mr. Johnson approached me, and said, "Sylvia, how'd you like to buy the restaurant from me?" I told Mr. Johnson that I didn't have

Kenneth and Bedelia in front of the beauty parlor in Hemingway, about 1958.

that kind of money saved, which I didn't, and Mr. Johnson said, "But doesn't your mother own some property down in Hemingway?"

"Yes, sir."

"So why not ask her for the money? She can mortgage her farm."

And that is exactly what she did. It was 1962—the beginning of Sylvia's Restaurant™.

All Through the Seasons

When I was a girl, every single thing we ate was either grown ourselves on the farm or traded with someone else for something they grew on theirs. Seeing as that I am now seventy-two years old, this was a long time ago, back before our farmhouse had electricity. Now, of course, things have changed a great deal. However, we pride ourselves on continuing to serve up delicious dishes of fresh vegetables in the restaurant. And when you can't get out to eat, we have our own line of delicious prepared soul food—vegetables, sauces, mixes, gravies, soups, and spices—that can be found on many supermarket shelves under the name Sylvia's Restaurant™: Queen of Soul Food™. That's me in the picture on the label, if you weren't sure.

But when I was young, things weren't so convenient. We ate fresh what was in season, and canned and preserved the rest ourselves, in the kitchen located a few yards away from the house. In the early part of the century, kitchens were not usually built as a room in a house. They were built separately so that during the blistering summers, the heat from the woodstove wouldn't come into the house.

We had all kinds of wonderful things to eat. In summer there were fresh sweet corn and tomatoes, tiny green beans, tender young collard greens, baby lima beans, butter beans in all colors, and plenty of just-picked field peas, which we ate fresh with their snaps. If you've never had field peas and snaps, I'm sorry to say that you have missed a great treat. We would gather the field peas off the vines in great handfuls, and sometimes, along with the fully ripe peas, we'd grab some of the immature pea shoots, too. These are called snaps; they look a little like snow peas. You'd eat the snaps and the peas together, after cooking them in water with a little bit of salt pork or ham. They were so delicious!

A lot of people call field peas "cow peas." That's because after you do all your picking in the pea fields, you let your cows in to graze. This way, nothing is wasted. We would eat as many of the freshly picked field peas as we could, and the rest would be dried and stored in cloth sacks for the winter. But before we could dry them, we would have to shell them. This would have taken a long time, if it weren't for a certain trick. You'd place the peas in a croaker sack, then beat them with a stick to loosen the shells. Then you'd hold a dishpan of the peas up high over your head, and slowly drop them onto a sheet on the ground. The wind would push the shells away from the beans as they fell. You could do this only on a windy day, but we had enough of those down south.

Apart from all the vegetables, we grew plenty of fruits back in Hemingway, too. There were pear, apple, and peach trees, a whole forest full of blackberries and blueberries waiting to be picked, and sweet black grapes growing in the grape arbor. But all the children loved watermelon best. In the summer, we used to eat watermelon almost every day. Sometimes the kids would burst open the melons in the fields and just scoop the hearts out with their hands, leaving the hard seeds behind.

My uncle Pete, who was my mother's brother-in-law, had a watermelon patch on his property. Although we had one on ours, we were devilish kids and

Crizette (right) *and her cousin Laura on*
Christmas Eve, about 1972. We managed to get the children into
their Christmas pjs, but they were too excited to go to bed.

preferred to sneak into his patch and steal his watermelons. Now, Pete was an old man when we stole his watermelons, and he would get so mad! He used to go and sit in the watermelon patch with his gun across his chest, watching for us. But after a little while, he would fall asleep. Then we'd sneak in and steal the melons. He slept right through it all—didn't even know we were in the patch.

Watermelon was more than a fruit, it was practically a game. I remember it being a favorite pastime while we were curing the tobacco in the summer. Someone would bring in a few watermelons and we would all eat them, letting the juice cool us down from the hard work and the heat of the furnace, which was turned up to 110°F to dry out the stems of the tobacco leaves. Sometimes, we wouldn't have a knife handy, but that didn't stop us from eating those watermelons. You would just take a melon and give it a good bang with the side of your hand, like a karate chop. The melon would split right open.

After all the tobacco was harvested and cured, there was cause for celebration. There'd be a big feast on the farm, and all the neighbors would come, bringing their best dishes. There was always mountains of food—some kind of perlow, maybe chicken, maybe sausage, a baked ham or barbecued ribs, potato salad, macaroni salad, collard or turnip greens, tomatoes and corn, baby lima beans with salt pork, candied yams, peas and rice, and many kinds of desserts, from butter cake to berry pie to apple cobbler and even homemade vanilla ice cream, which was churned the old-fashioned way in a wooden bucket surrounded by rock salt and plenty of ice. We drank iced tea and lemonade and someone might have been passing a jug of homemade corn liquor around to the men, but I never knew much about that as a girl. We stayed up late, happy that the hardest work for the harvest was done. My family harvested everything from that forty-acre farm ourselves. My grandmother even had me out in the fields picking cotton when I was six years old, which was usual for the time. Along with tobacco, we grew corn and cotton. Those were the three big money crops. Believe me, once those were harvested, packed, and ready to be sold, we were always in the mood to celebrate.

Labor Day, which marked the official end of summer and the return to school for the children, was another reason for us to celebrate. To this day, the family drives down to South Carolina to celebrate there, like we've done ever since I can remember. The way my family celebrates Labor Day, it's just one big party all weekend long. From the moment we unpack the cars until we set out on the road again a few days later, we go from one feast to the next without interruption.

One of our favorite meals to eat together around the holidays is breakfast.

My family in front of the restaurant: Kenneth, his wife, Sylvia, Herbert,
Crizette, me, Bedelia, and Van.

My granddaughters Sibeanna and Trenness.

When my mother was alive, she kept plenty of spots, a type of fish, on hand so that she could fry them up in the morning for us to eat with grits, tomatoes and okra, biscuits, and syrup. We always had two kinds of syrup in the house—Alagra, which was made from sorghum, and Cane Patch syrup, which was made from sugarcane. Mama had to keep baking biscuits all morning long, because once we started eating, everybody would reach for two or three biscuits.

When we gathered around the breakfast table, my mother would let each one of the children, even the littlest, say a short prayer, and then share with us a bit about how their lives had changed since the last time they got up to the table. It's a tradition that Herbert and I carry on to this day. We like to hear what the young ones have to say. When the children are done with their prayers, Herbert and I speak. We let our children, grandchildren, and even great-grandchildren know how good they are, how much we appreciate them growing up the way they are growing—spiritually and otherwise. These prayers make up a deeply important family ritual that helps all of us stay close to one another. Before she passed from this earth, my mother would always make the last prayer, asking God to bless our whole family. Now, Herbert and I say this closing prayer. And then we eat.

It almost seems that right after breakfast, we all have to go somewhere and start getting ready for the next meal. On Labor Day, there are usually several celebrations to attend, including my cousin Dolly's barbecue and the church picnic. Everyone contributes some of our favorite soul food dishes—barbecued and fried chicken, potato salad, macaroni and cheese, collard greens, beans and rice, candied yams, green beans, okra, and butter beans. There are also hot dogs, hamburgers, and, on the Monday, Labor Day itself, barbecued venison and raccoon, made by my cousin Dolly. Kenneth especially loves Dolly's venison and 'coon,

Van, 1945.

and he always makes sure to pack a few 'coon sandwiches for the car ride back.

Once Labor Day was over, when I was a young girl, we began getting ourselves ready for the winter. Now, if you are from the North, you may not believe that it could get that cold in South Carolina, but let me tell you, it does! Especially since the houses weren't heated and insulated like they are now. The bedrooms were especially cold, because the only heat came from a fireplace in the living room. Sometimes we would heat our supper by that fireplace. But before making a fire, we would have to gather the logs from the woods. That was our job on Saturdays—to take the mule and the wagon and go out and haul a load of wood to the house for the week.

On the coldest nights, all the grown-ups would sit around close to the warmth of the fire and tell stories, about themselves and about other people in town, too. We children would play off to the side of the fire, and although we weren't supposed to be listening, we heard every word. Children are curious; they may be playing, but they are listening, too. We heard a whole lot that we shouldn't have. But since no one wanted to send us to bed in the cold, my mother and grandmother let us stay up until we were so sleepy we had to go to bed. When I look back on it all now, it seems like life would have been such a struggle. But back then, we didn't know about central heat and electricity and indoor kitchens and bathrooms. You can't miss what you never had. And besides, we always had the warmth of our family's love to keep us cozy inside and out. There's not much more you can ask for than that.

Since the winter months were cold, that's when everyone would do their slaughtering. Back before anyone had freezers and refrigerators, the cold air helped keep the meat fresh, until we could either salt it down, preserve it, or eat it.

Before we had freezers of our own, we had to bring the butchered meat to

My son Van and his family (clockwise from top left): *Vonet, Che, Shauna, Sierra, Van, Malaika, and Brenda (Van's wife), holding DeVaughn.*

*Bedelia in 1948, in the park near our apartment
on 131st Street in Harlem.*

town to store in the Hemingway Freezer. This was not a freezer in the modern sense of the word. It was like a giant meat locker, and everyone paid to keep their meat in a small compartment which was kept cold with ice. About once a week or so, whenever we wanted to eat something other than chicken (which we killed fresh ourselves) or meat from the smokehouse (like salt pork, sausages, and hams), we went to the freezer and took out some of our supply.

Whenever we or one of our neighbors had to go into town to do an errand, like getting meat out of the freezer, we would make sure to ask all the families on the lane if they needed anything. To do this, we didn't even have to leave our porch. You see, before anyone had a telephone, we used to communicate by calling out to each other across the fields. The houses were about forty yards apart, and the only things in between were the cotton or tobacco fields. So the ladies could all stand on their porches and hold long conversations with one another. We would talk about anything, chat about the weather, about our kids and husbands. I mean, someone would call out, "Mama, do you have any flour over there, because I am trying to fix these kids something to eat?" We would talk as we went about what we were doing, like shelling the beans or, if one lady was in the middle of cooking something, she would run into the kitchen, saying, "I'll be right back, let me go and finish cooking up the such and such." Then she would come back and we would finish our conversation. It's amazing how well our voices carried over the fields!

Of course, there were times that we didn't want to call out to each other, maybe because we had something private to say, or because it was getting late and we didn't want to wake the littlest children, or because it was winter and

Herbert, me, and Bedelia at the restaurant, about 1973.

therefore too cold to stand out on the porch. Then we had to send a messenger. One of the older kids got that job, but they never seemed to mind because they got to see their cousins or friends down the lane.

That's the thing with having the whole family living in little houses right near each other. Our fields were almost like a family compound. Whenever someone got married and needed to build a little house, they would do it on the family farm. And this is part of what made our community so strong. The children were not just raised by their own parents, they were raised by the whole town, and there was always someone watching out for them, even if their parents were working or at the store or inside the house. The children had to behave themselves because all the adults knew each child, and wouldn't hesitate to say something if a child needed scolding or tell the parents if a child needed to be punished for some little childish crime. It was what made our children grow up to be responsible, hardworking people. It really does take a whole village to raise a child.

So it wasn't just on holidays that all the families went from one relative's house to another. It was every day, with the children running here and there, visiting their friends and delivering our messages. On Sundays, the adults got to visit with one another, too. After church was over, we would cluster in small groups, talking and catching up on the week. Sometimes, different members of our extended family and dear friends would get together and share Sunday dinner. When my mother was alive, she made Sunday dinner at her house, and would invite different people to come by. There were usually at least ten people sitting around her dining table, and even more on Sundays when the preacher and his wife would join us.

My mama would always have chicken on Sundays. Everyone in Hemingway did. No matter how poor a family was, there was a chicken in every pot on Sunday. Sometimes my mother fried it, sometimes she roasted it or smothered it, but it would be there as the centerpiece of the meal along with one other kind of meat. On Sunday, Mama made two meats—chicken, plus maybe a ham or pork roast or beef stew. She would start cooking early in the morning before church, then finish up right before people started arriving. Even now I can remember those wonderful smells drifting out of her kitchen—the tender cornbread and biscuits baking, the chicken frying in a black iron pan, the macaroni and cheese, and the sweet scent of a layer cake in the oven or maybe a pot full of custard for banana pudding. My mother made delicious meals every single day of the week, and she really went to town on Sundays.

But even on weekdays, dinnertime was a special ritual. When I was a girl, and even when my children were growing up in Hemingway, every member of the family ate together every single day. And, unlike what most people do today, we all ate the same thing, and dinner lasted for a few hours. We never just swallowed our food and excused ourselves from the table. It wasn't allowed. No, dinnertime was when the family really got a chance to talk and to communicate with one another. No matter what people were feeling or doing before they sat down, no matter if so-and-so was angry with someone else, everyone put their tensions behind them and came to the dinner table feeling good. Dinnertime was real family time, a time for all of us to share our thoughts with one another and to share a wonderful meal that my mother had made.

Although my mother tried to make every single meal special, there was no meal so special as Christmas dinner. This was my mother's time to make all our favorite dishes at once, and the preparations took her weeks. She began right after Thanksgiving, when she had all the children help her crack nuts and churn butter for the dozens and dozens of cakes and pies she baked, and continued right up until the time that everyone started coming to her door on Christmas Eve.

But like every other holiday, at Christmas we travel from house to house, seeing all our relatives. Now that my mother is no longer with us we usually go to Herbert's sister Bertha's house to share in her festivities. We always stop by my cousin Tennie's house, too, to see that part of the family. No matter how far away everyone has moved from Hemingway, we all come home at Christmas.

When I was growing up, we used to have a live Christmas tree every year. Most families did back then. And we didn't have to buy a tree, either. We'd just go find one in the woods. All the neighbors would go tree hunting together, since we needed help carrying the trees back to the houses. We would walk into the woods and the children would run around and look at all the trees. Whenever someone saw a likely candidate, the men would come and chop it down. Once we got our tree home, we decorated it with big pinecones we found in the woods and with plenty of silvery angel's hair. Under the tree would go the presents, but they weren't put out until Santa brought them on Christmas Eve.

It was very hard getting the children to go to bed on Christmas Eve. I remember when I was a girl how excited I would be, waiting until I could tear open my presents on Christmas morning. And my children were the same way when they were little. To make them go to sleep, we told them what our parents had told us— that Santa Claus would put pepper into the eyes of any children who were awake when he came down the chimney with their gifts. It definitely got them to go to bed, but it also made all the children somewhat scared of Santa.

One year, we bought a Santa Claus suit. This was when all the kids were grown-up except for Crizette, who was still little enough to believe in Santa and his pepper. As soon as she, and Bedelia's son Lindsay, who was about the same age, saw Kenneth in that Santa suit, they got so terrified that they hid under the bed until "Santa" went away. Once the kids got too old to believe in Santa, someone in the family dressed up in the Santa suit and we would all drive around the town, waving at the children and giving out pieces of fruit. Some of the neighborhood kids were scared then, too.

There was one year when Crizette was still a child that Santa Claus didn't make it to our house at all! Kenneth was picked to be Santa that year, and that meant that as soon as Crizette and the other children were asleep, he was supposed to take the presents out of the car (we had brought them down from New York) and put them under the tree. Well, this year, Kenneth had stayed out late with his friends, and ended up drinking a little too much eggnog. He came home and fell asleep, forgetting all about the presents. The next morning when Crizette and the other children woke up, they cried, "Santa Claus didn't send us anything! Santa Claus forgot about us!" Crizette was especially upset, crying and protesting, "But I was good, I promise, I was good all year!" That's when Crizette knew for sure that there was no Santa Claus. There was only her brother, sleeping off his bellyful of holiday cheer.

Our Children, Our Future

Ever since I was a little girl, there was nothing that I wanted more than a family full of children and grandchildren. Now, I have my wish; we are the proud parents of four children, grandparents of sixteen, great-grandparents of two, and godparents of two, all beautiful, intelligent, good people who make us thankful that God has blessed my family in such a wonderful way.

All four of our children, Van, Bedelia, Kenneth, and Crizette, are involved in the restaurant, and each one lends the business his or her own individual talents.

They are the future of Sylvia's Restaurant™, and when Herbert and I pass from this earth, I know they will continue running it in ways that could only make us even more proud of them than we already are.

Van is our firstborn child. He was born on January 7, 1945, when I was eighteen years old. Herbert and I had been married for almost a year. We got married on January 18, 1944, and sometimes I think that Van was trying to beat our anniversary. Herbert was overseas in the navy when Van was born. In her role as a midwife, my grandmother delivered the baby on our living-room floor at about eleven in the morning. I named him after my father.

I have to say that since Van was our first baby, I remember every detail about

Bedelia and her daughter, Tamicka.

Bedelia's son, Lindsay.   *Kenneth's youngest son, Marcus.*

his birth. Once the labor and delivery were over, my grandmother took one look at her new great-grandchild and said, "Oh, my God, this baby has a veil over his face. He's going to be a lucky child." A veil is a thin tissue that children are sometimes born with. You have to pull it off. Some people consider children born with a veil to be lucky, and my grandmother was one of them. I guess they thought that if a baby can survive that, he can survive anything.

Anyway, before Herbert returned from sea, Van was the only male in the house. I was living with my mother in the rooms behind the beauty parlor, and my grandmother was living across the fields in her house. So in September, when Herbert returned, Van didn't know what to make of this strange man who was trying to take away his mother's attention. Van was a very, very jealous nine-month-old. When his daddy would come sit by me or put his arm around me, little baby Van would push him away or try to get in between Herbert and me if we embraced.

Then he would scream at the top of his lungs and say in a real loud baby voice, "NO!"

It took a while before Herbert found a way to get Van to realize who he was. He would stand Van on a table in front of a mirror and stand next to him. Van would start out crying, and Herbert would point to his face and Van's face until he would stop crying and begin to see the resemblance between the two of them. Once that happened, they became inseparable. And later, instead of following me around, he'd follow Herbert around.

Ever since Van was a little boy, he had a special kind of intelligence and a real vision. He was always looking for something, seeking out something, like pulling books off the shelf and trying to read them, or finding records and listening to music over and over. Van was always a leader. He used to fight a lot when he was in school because he couldn't stand injustice. If he saw a bigger kid taking advantage of his cousin Alex, he would get in between the kids and fight in Alex's place. Van had the reputation of being a good fighter, and no one wanted to get him angry. On the flip side, Van was also a very loyal friend and a protective older brother. Kenneth remembers that if he ever got into trouble at school, Van would come to his aid. Kenneth admits that he worshiped the ground his older brother walked on.

By the time I bought the restaurant, Van was in high school. He didn't get involved in the business until much later, after he had graduated from college with a degree in marketing. But first he went to work in other companies. Then Van decided to come to work with us. This is how he tells it: "It was later in my

Me and Herbert with Kenneth, his wife, Sylvia, and his three children,
Kendra, Marcus, and DeSean.

Me and Van with our line of delicious soul food products.

life that I got the vision of how my family could expand the business and start our own specialty food line. But believe me, it wasn't easy. It took a lot to turn things around. When we decided to modernize the restaurant, expand, and clean up the block, we ran into some challenges. Mother was always focused on making sure that her customers had good food and quality service, even while we were going through the remodeling. I hope to do for our business what my mother means for soul food."

And Van has certainly left his mark. He is the one who thought of acquiring real estate and of enlarging the restaurant to take up almost the whole block, like it does now. He was also the one who put the work into developing our line of specially seasoned, quality prepared foods, the Sylvia's Restaurant™: Queen of Soul Food™ products, which are available in supermarkets across the country. Van has a lot of life and, whenever he is involved in a project, you know it will happen—Van has the important combination of vision and follow-through.

Bedelia, our first daughter, was born three years after Van, in 1949. Herbert and I were living in Harlem at the time, and I had Bedelia in the apartment we were living in on 131st Street. From the time she was born, Bedelia was always a loving, sweet baby, but she also had a mind of her own. She was a little bit of a loner as a child. She preferred to stay in her room, finding ways to play all afternoon by herself. I never had to worry about her because she was so good and self-sufficient.

Now, Bedelia, like Van, was a teenager when I opened the restaurant, just getting ready to go to high school. Part of Bedelia's responsibility was to help out in the restaurant after school in order to earn her spending money. I guess, secretly, it was my way of keeping tabs on her. A lot of things were changing very fast in Harlem, and I was really concerned that my working in the restaurant made it difficult to keep up with her. Bedelia adjusted fairly well. Her schoolmates would come by, give her a hand while she was working behind the counter; they'd usually eat for free; and when she'd finish her chores, she'd have some money to go out.

But when Bedelia got ready to get her first job, she didn't want to work at the restaurant. Her first job was at Chock Full o'Nuts. Some of my customers saw her there and asked her why she was working there instead of the restaurant. She eventually came back. By then she had learned so much, and she used what she knew to help us expand our business, which she did by developing Sylvia's catering. In fact, I think that starting the catering business was Bedelia's idea in the first place.

This wouldn't come as a surprise to anyone who knows how creative Bedelia is and what a hard worker she is. The idea to add a catering business to our restaurant flowed naturally from Bedelia's own love of entertaining and of cooking. There is nothing that pleases Bedelia so much as having all her friends and family over and cooking up a huge meal. She is the one gathering up everybody to go on picnics. Then she would have reason to cook everyone's favorite foods, like candied yams, steaks, barbecued ribs and chicken, and pigs' feet. She also makes breakfast at her home before a picnic, so that she can have company while she gets the food ready for later. While she has the ribs and chicken in the oven, and the pigs' feet boiling in a pot, she may also be frying fish or making French toast to serve for breakfast. Bedelia is good at doing a million things at once.

In addition to being a terrific picnic thrower, Bedelia is an inventive cook and likes to create new recipes by combining the flavors of the soul food she grew up eating with a lighter, more healthful cooking style. She has greatly influenced the menu at the restaurant in this way, bringing it more in line with the current marketplace. It was Bedelia who suggested that we add a few lighter dishes for health-conscious eaters to our menu, like grilled chicken breast and salad.

I think that Bedelia has inherited a lot of my traits, especially in terms of her warmth and hospitality.

Our third child, Kenneth, was born in 1953. Of the four children, Kenneth grew up just as much in Hemingway, with my mother, as he did in Harlem. He spent a great deal of time during his formative years moving between New York and the South, attending school in both places. Kenneth was very close to my mother, Julia, and probably has more of her ways and her sayings than anyone else. Mama taught him to fish, hunt, drive, and all of the social graces. She also taught him, like she taught all the children, how to be responsible, honest, and strong in his life, and these are lessons that Kenneth, in particular, seemed to take to heart. Whether it's because of my mother, or just because he is who he is, Kenneth has grown into a very moral, upstanding, and trustworthy man.

He is also a born storyteller, and can take any moment in his life and give it a dramatic and funny spin in the retelling. One story that Kenneth often tells is about when he finally learned that it was much easier to do his chores and obey his grandmother than it was not to. And my mama definitely kept those children busy, with stripping and mending the lines, helping make dinner, shelling beans, sweeping floors, running errands, washing up after meals, clearing the table. Everyone, no matter how small, helped. Kenneth always meant well; it wasn't that he didn't want to do his chores, but there were times when he forgot, especially when he was playing outside.

Here's how Kenneth tells the story of his very last punishment: "My grandma, she had a way of making sure no matter how small the crime was, everything got treated the same. There were no big wrongs or little wrongs.

And because of that, you were just as likely to get whipped for not doing your chores as you were for doing something worse, like skipping school. Well, when I was eight or nine, I decided that I never wanted to get punished again. I had forgotten to do some kind of chore—I think I didn't feed the chickens one day—and after supper, when I was getting ready for bed, Grandma came up to me and asked me why I hadn't fed the chickens. I told her that I forgot, and she whipped me. Afterward, I said, 'This is it, Grandma, I am not getting whipped anymore.'

"And I kept that promise, because from that day on when she told me to feed the chickens, I would feed the chickens, feed the hogs, dust the furniture, wax the furniture, sweep the floor. I would do things just to make her happy. And I never got punished again."

But even though Kenny got punished every now and then, he really loved his grandma, who was like a second mother to him. He had a way of getting her to play with him so you would think she was much younger than she actually was. After a whole day of working, delivering babies, or checking on new mothers, she would still find the time to play with little Kenneth and the other children. "You want to race?" she would ask him, and then he and his cousins would go outside and they would all race, including Mama. Or she would say, "Do you want to exercise?" and then she would see if everyone could touch their toes without bending their knees, and other things like that. She would do all of this, even though she was on the heavy side, to please the children, and Kenneth basked in all the attention.

Another thing that my mother passed down to Kenneth is his love of the out-doors. Kenneth is quite a sportsman, a champion fisherman, and an expert hunter. I think that there is probably nothing that Kenneth likes more than being outdoors and communing with nature. That's why he is especially happy visiting South Car-

A lovely photo of Crizette, when she was eighteen.

olina, where he can hunt and fish to his heart's delight. But even when he's in New York, in between working at the restaurant and spending time with his family, he can usually find a few hours in which he can take a boat out to fish, if the season is right. That's the thing about Kenneth; he can combine his responsibilities with his pleasures, and make everyone, including himself, happy and satisfied.

Crizette, our youngest child, was practically born in the restaurant. This was in 1967, five years after we had bought the place from Mr. Johnson. You see, when I started having labor pains—we were living in the Bronx then—I told Herbert to drive me to the restaurant before taking me to Women's Hospital, where Crizette was eventually born. By this time, the restaurant had become such a part of me that I couldn't imagine going anywhere without stopping by first. So I came to the restaurant, and was checking up on things when Sally, one of our waitresses, said, "Sylvia, please, get out of here before that baby is born in this restaurant!" But still, I didn't want to go. I had delivered all the other children in my home and had never been to a hospital before. I was understandably scared. Finally, Herbert dragged me into the car and we drove to the hospital.

After Crizette was born, I came back to work very soon, bringing my tiny baby with me. I would wrap her in blankets and put her in the bread drawer under the counter, where it was warm and snug and I could keep my eyes on her while I worked. When she outgrew the bread box, I pushed one of the booths up to the wall to form a crib and watched her from there. She is the only one of the children who I can say really grew up in the restaurant—even before she was old enough to remember.

When Crizette turned four or five, I took her to a day-care center around the corner from the restaurant. When I picked her up in the afternoon and brought her back, I would feed her and then let her clear her own plates off the table. After she got accustomed to doing that, I would then let her clear off someone else's table by saying, "You see how you took your plates off? Now go get theirs, too." And she would. She eventually began to help clear off the tables in the restaurant. Then I put her behind the counter to take orders or in the kitchen to help wash dishes.

Crizette was such a wonderful, adorable baby. After Herbert and I would come home from a day's work, Crizette—she must have been about two—would run to the door and bring us our house slippers. She maybe had one foot of mine and one foot of his, but she would always meet us at the door with our slippers. This kind of foresight and thoughtfulness has remained with her to this day, and she is really one of the most observant, sensitive, and loving people I know, with a heart as big and generous as any you can imagine.

When Crizette was a small child, Herbert and I decided that she should spend her summers down in South Carolina with my mother and Kenneth, who was living down there most of the year. I wanted her to learn the lessons that my mother had to teach. Mama had those kids working hard around the house, doing chores and such, but she also spoiled them, especially Crizette, who was the baby. Crizette always loved the crispy skin from my mother's fried chicken, and Mama would take off the skin from her own piece to give to Crizette.

Crizette and her oldest daughter, Zaqura. *Crizette and her husband, Mike, at the wedding.*

But, as much as she loved being with her grandmother, Crizette was more of a city child and preferred staying in New York with her friends to dividing her time between two places. When she was about eleven, we let her stay in New York for the summer, where she went to camp during the day, then worked at the restaurant in the afternoons. She did a little of everything, washing the dishes, taking orders, hostessing. And the customers loved her, since most of the regulars knew her from when she was an infant.

Crizette is now involved in all phases of managing and running the restaurant, including the cooking and preparation of food for regular and special events. With Crizette working at the restaurant, she has completed the cycle of all my children growing up, leaving home, and then deciding, on their own, to come back into the fold. Each one offers their own particular gifts to running Sylvia's, and altogether they make a mama proud.

Warming Soups and Relishes

Whenever I think of soup, I think of New Year's Eve. Actually, I don't really think of New Year's Eve, I think of New Year's Day, which is also the day my mother was born. You see, where I come from in Hemingway, New Year's Eve is a time to really have a good time with the family. First, everyone went to church to pray for a healthy and happy new year and to give thanks for the past year. Then, when Herbert and I were younger, we used to go to a few parties. But no matter what, we'd always end up at my brother McKinley's house to bring in the new year. I can remember many a year when Herbert and I would rush into McKinley's, breathless and panting, just as the countdown to midnight began. Then we'd stay there for the rest of the night until morning came, which is what everyone did back then. We had some good times.

Anyway, once we finally got home, that's when we ate our New Year's Day soup. We didn't have one particular kind, just whatever I had made in advance. That's the thing about eating soup on New Year's Day. You could make it in advance, then heat it up in the morning. It was always so warming, which a body craves, since it's a cold time of year. Soup gives you strength to get through the day, which we needed, since we hadn't slept the night before and we had to be up to take care of the family.

Of course, this is not to say that we didn't eat soup during the rest of the year. We ate it all the time in cold weather, and even in the warm weather when one of us was sick. Nothing makes a sick person well as quickly as a bowl of chicken soup. My mother, taking after my grandmother, used to put pots of chicken soup on to simmer in the kitchens of women who had just given birth. That soup would fortify the new mother in those days after childbirth.

When I was working at Johnson's luncheonette before it became Sylvia's Restaurant™, we used to have a soup lunch special Monday through Friday. It attracted all the workers at the gas company and telephone company, who'd come in for lunch when those offices were up on 125th Street. We called the special "a bowl and a roll." You got a bowl of soup, which changed each day of the week, and a hard, seeded roll, all for about 65 cents. Remember, this was in the 1950s. Anyway, I remember that the beef vegetable soup was a particular favorite, since it was filling enough to last all afternoon long.

Chicken Soup | *Makes 6 to 8 servings*

There's nothing that heals the body and mind as a bowl of steaming hot chicken soup. My grandmother, who was a midwife, always made sure that if any of her ladies gave birth at night, by the next morning there was a stewed hen in that new mother's pot. Stewed hen and chicken soup would nurse anyone back to life.

For this recipe, if you can get an old hen, use it to make the broth. It will have more flavor that way.

1 ½ pounds chicken wings

6 cups water

2 cups chopped tomato

1 cup chopped onion

1 cup sliced carrot

¾ cup chopped celery

½ cup chopped green bell pepper

1 tablespoon parsley flakes

1 ½ teaspoons salt

1 teaspoon poultry seasoning

1 teaspoon sugar

½ teaspoon freshly ground black pepper

¼ teaspoon hot sauce

¼ teaspoon garlic salt

Place the chicken wings in a 4-quart pot. Add the remaining ingredients. Bring to a boil over high heat. Reduce the heat and simmer, uncovered, for 1 hour.

Beef Vegetable Soup | *Makes 8 to 10 servings*

Whenever my grandmother butchered one of her cows, she would make sure to save the backbone for making soup. Since cows were usually slaughtered around February, we would always look forward to her simmering that backbone into a pot of rich beef vegetable soup. Now this recipe was something that she usually served us for supper, not for dinner. You see, in the country, dinner was the main meal of the day, and it was served around noon. Supper was a light meal and it was served around 6:00. This soup is not as hearty as the beef stew recipe, and is just the thing to eat as a light meal in the depth of winter. Nowadays, we also serve it for lunch.

1 quart water

1 pound stewing beef, cut into small pieces

1 tablespoon Worcestershire sauce

1 1/2 teaspoons salt

1/2 teaspoon freshly ground black pepper

1/4 teaspoon dried thyme

2 bay leaves

2 cups chopped cabbage

2 cups chopped tomato

1 cup chopped carrot

1 cup chopped onion

1 cup chopped green bell pepper

2/3 cup chopped celery

1/2 cup diced turnip

2 tablespoons chopped celery leaves (optional)

2 cups diced potato

1/4 cup elbow macaroni

1. In a 6-quart pot bring the water, beef, Worcestershire sauce, salt, black pepper, thyme, and bay leaves to a boil. Reduce the heat and simmer, covered, for 1 hour.

2. Add the cabbage, tomato, carrot, onion, bell pepper, celery, turnip, and celery leaves. Return to a boil. Reduce the heat and simmer, covered, for 2 hours longer. Add the potato and macaroni and simmer, uncovered, for 30 minutes longer. Discard the bay leaves before serving.

Creamy Zucchini Soup

My husband, Herbert, is very fond of zucchini, and probably has a million ways of preparing it. I know that most people don't think of zucchini when they think of soup. Neither did I, but Herbert loved it so much that I had to learn to prepare it for him. And it's such a rich, thick, savory soup that it makes a perfect light supper on one of those cold winter nights that we spend together in our home in Mount Vernon, New York.

3 cups sliced zucchini

1 ½ cups chicken broth (one 14 ½-ounce can)

½ cup chopped onion

⅓ cup chopped green bell pepper

1 ½ teaspoons lemon pepper seasoning

1 ½ teaspoons sugar

½ teaspoon salt

¼ teaspoon poultry seasoning

¼ teaspoon hot sauce

¼ teaspoon freshly ground black pepper

2 tablespoons butter

2 tablespoons all-purpose flour

1 ½ cups half-and-half

One 7-ounce can corn kernels, undrained

1. In a 1½-quart saucepan, combine the zucchini, broth, onion, bell pepper, lemon pepper seasoning, sugar, salt, poultry seasoning, hot sauce, and black pepper. Bring to a boil over high heat. Reduce the heat and simmer for 20 minutes or until the vegetables are soft.

2. In a 2-quart saucepan, melt the butter over medium heat. Add the flour and stir until absorbed. Using a whisk, stir in the half-and-half until there are no lumps of flour. Stir in the zucchini-broth mixture and the corn with the canning liquid. Bring to a boil, stirring frequently. Reduce the heat and simmer for 2 minutes.

"You Can't Eat Just One" Snackin' Crackers

Makes 6 cups or 12 (or considerably fewer) servings

Frances Donnelly

This recipe from my sister-in-law Frances is positively addictive. Whenever she puts a big bowl of snackin' crackers out during the holidays, they disappear, even though everyone claims to have eaten just one or two. But it's easy to lose count when something is this good.

Frances says that you can make these crackers in advance and store them in a covered bowl in the refrigerator. I say that if you do make them ahead, there might not be any left over when you want to serve them.

¹/₄ cup vegetable oil

One 1-ounce package dry ranch dressing dip

¹/₂ teaspoon dill weed

¹/₂ teaspoon garlic powder

¹/₂ teaspoon lemon pepper

One 10- or 11-ounce package oyster crackers

1. In a large bowl, stir together the oil, ranch dressing, dill weed, garlic powder, and lemon pepper.

2. Add the crackers and toss until completely coated.

Ruby Love's Pickled Okra | *Makes 5½ cups or 24 to 30 servings*

Ruby Love Dulan

Ruby Love Dulan, the mother of a friend of ours, sent along this unique recipe for pickled okra. Although I use okra in all kinds of traditional soul food dishes—in stews and gumbos, cooked with butter beans or tomatoes, or just fried—I'd never made it into a pickle before I saw this recipe. Ruby Love wrote that you can spike up the flavor by adding some red pepper to the brine. Pearl onions are also good here. Even if you don't sterilize the jars, the pickle will still keep in the refrigerator for about a month.

2 pounds fresh okra

3 cups distilled white vinegar

1 ½ cups water

1 ½ tablespoons salt

½ cup chopped fresh dill

1 ½ tablespoons dill seed

1. Rinse and drain the okra, snipping off the very tip of the stem, if necessary, but not removing the cap. Stand the okra in 3 sterilized pint jars, following jar directions for safe canning procedures.

2. Combine the vinegar, water, and salt in a 2-quart saucepan. Bring to a boil over high heat. Boil for 5 minutes. Add the dill and dill seed and boil for 2 minutes longer.

3. Pour the hot vinegar and water mixture over the okra, covering the okra, but leaving a 1-inch head space in the jar. Place the sterilized lids on the jars and refrigerate for 1 week before serving. Store in the refrigerator.

Venice's Sliced Cucumber Pickles

Makes 5½ cups or 20 servings

Venice Singletary

As I mentioned earlier, before we had refrigeration, we used the old-fashioned method of canning and preserving in mason jars. We canned everything we could, from pickled pigs' feet to greens, tomatoes, corn, and beans, to pears, apples, grapes, and watermelon. We would store these colorful jars of preserves in the smokehouse, and they would last us all winter long until the garden got going again. Although not many people can much anymore, our friend Venice Singletary still makes these wonderful cucumber pickles. Although she cans them the old-fashioned way, you can simply store them in the refrigerator. They will keep for at least a month—if they last that long.

12 cups sliced Kirby cucumbers
2 cups sliced onion
2 cups cider vinegar
2 cups sugar
3 tablespoons salt
1 teaspoon celery seeds
1 teaspoon mustard seeds
1 teaspoon ground turmeric

1. In a large nonmetallic bowl, layer the cucumber slices with the onion.

2. In a 2-quart container, stir together the cider vinegar, sugar, and salt until the sugar dissolves. Stir in the celery seeds, mustard seeds, and turmeric. Pour over the cucumber slices and onion. Cover with plastic wrap and let stand at room temperature for 1 week, stirring occasionally. Store in the refrigerator.

Chicken and Turkey

Back in Hemingway, we raised all our own poultry, and my mother had quite a collection of birds scraping around the back of the house and in front of the chicken coop. On the outside of the chicken coop, each hen had her own little nest, which was a little pile of hay and straw placed in one of the little cubby-holes along the walls. Chickens always go back to the same nest to lay, so you knew which chickens were the best layers. In my mother's coop, it was the Rhode Island Reds, which were bought special for laying. We could check for eggs in the morning. Back then, we ate eggs every which way—for breakfast, dinner, and supper, fried with sausage, scrambled with ham or bacon, made into cakes, pies, and puddings. I can still remember how good those yellow farm eggs would taste cooked on the same day as they were laid.

Then there were the turkeys, which laid big, beige eggs. My mother got the turkey chicks from a lady she knew, and before long, we had a whole flock. She also raised guineas. Those are strange-looking birds with fat bodies and long necks. They originated in Africa, and I know that some people call them African turkeys. Anyway, they had the sweetest meat. My mother used to stew them, since they were a little bit tough, but they sure were sweet.

Taking care of all the poultry was extremely important on the farm, and the birds had to be fed once a day. When the chicks are babies, you feed them ground corn. Once they get a little bigger, they get cracked corn, and the full-grown chickens get whole corn. Back then we got the corn from the field, but today most people just buy it. When you'd go to feed the chickens, they would all gather around your legs, pecking where the corn fell.

One time, my mother got hit by lightning because of her chickens. It was a terrible stormy day, with thunder in the sky and the rain coming down so hard you could barely see. My mother ran out into the rain so that she could chase the chickens back into the coop. She was worried that the little chicks might drown in the puddles. So there she was, waving at the chicks and running behind them, when a slash of lightning came out of the sky and struck her down. But Mama was lucky; she managed to crawl into the house.

God was looking out for her on that day, and it was a miracle that she escaped with nothing but a big burn on her calf. It turned into a scar to remind her of God's grace. After that, my mother pretty well gave up the chickens.

Barbecued Chicken

Makes 2 to 4 servings

I have to say, barbecuing a chicken is not what I think of when I think of barbecue. In Hemingway, when you say barbecue, everyone knows you mean barbecued pig. We ate a lot of barbecued pork when I was growing up. But unless it was Christmas, we didn't barbecue a hog ourselves.

Instead, what we did was to slaughter the hog, then send it along to Rosie's at the Brunsen crossroads in town, where they would barbecue it for us. Serving barbecue was no spur of the moment kind of thing. We had to make the arrangements about a week in advance.

These days, with everyone thinking about their health, we barbecue all kinds of things, including turkey, which is now a big favorite on Thanksgiving and Christmas, and chicken, which is easy to make, delicious to eat, and perfect to serve on Sundays for dinner.

There's one trick to making this recipe, and that is the cider vinegar. Using two whole cups may sound like a lot, but it really makes the meat "falling-off-the-bone" tender.

One 3- to 4-pound chicken, cut into eighths

1 ½ teaspoons salt

1 ½ teaspoons freshly ground black pepper

2 cups cider vinegar

2 cups barbecue sauce of your choice

1. Preheat the oven to 350°F.

2. Season the chicken with the salt and pepper and let stand at least 20 minutes, or even better, overnight in the refrigerator. Arrange the pieces in a 9 × 13 × 2-inch baking pan. Add the vinegar. Bake, uncovered, for 45 minutes, turning once. Drain off most of the vinegar.

3. Pour the barbecue sauce over the chicken. Bake for 30 minutes longer.

Roast Chicken | *Makes 4 to 5 servings*

When I was growing up, we always had a chicken dinner on Sundays. Everyone in Hemingway did; no matter how rich or poor a family was, on Sunday, there was a chicken in every pot. At that time, most people cooked up one of their own chickens. My mother was no exception. Every Saturday, she would go out into the yard, select a likely candidate, and, well, you know the rest.

Mama would have to start her cooking for Sunday dinner early before church. Then all of us would walk over to Jeremiah, back when it was still a small, white wooden building. After church service, my mother would run back home to finish the cooking, especially if it was a day when the preacher was coming to eat with us.

We generally had at least ten people sitting around the table at our house, and that would include the children. We sat at the table with the adults and we shared the dinner equally. There were some families in which the adults would eat first and let the children eat later. Sometimes, the guests ate up all of the chicken, and it seemed as if there would be none left for the kids. But not in our house. No matter how many guests my mother had, she always made sure we had enough.

Roast chicken with cornbread stuffing was one of our favorite Sunday dinners. Although this recipe just calls for seasoning the bird with salt and pepper, Mama always massaged the seasonings into the skin, rubbing that chicken like it was a baby's bottom. Then she'd roast the chicken while we went to church. It was delicious.

One 4- to 5¹/₂-pound whole chicken
1 tablespoon salt
1 tablespoon poultry seasoning
1 ¹/₂ teaspoons freshly ground black pepper

¹/₄ cup (¹/₂ stick) butter, at room temperature
Cornbread Stuffing (page 219, or stuffing of your choice)

1. Preheat the oven to 350°F. Rinse the chicken thoroughly and pat dry.

2. In a small bowl, stir together the salt, poultry seasoning, and pepper. Sprinkle the salt mixture over the entire bird, inside and out. Let stand for at least 30 minutes or, even better, overnight in the refrigerator. Rub the chicken inside and out with the butter.

3. Fill the cavities of the bird with the stuffing and sew the skin of the openings closed (or use toothpicks to hold the skin together).

4. Place the chicken, breast side down, in a roasting pan. Bake for 1 hour. Turn the chicken breast side up and bake for 45 minutes to 1 hour longer or until the juices run clear when pricked with a fork.

Me and Herbert with Ike and Sallie Brown.

Van's Garlic Chicken | *Makes 4 servings*

Van and Brenda Woods

There's always someone knocking on my son Van's door to get his opinion and advice about something. You see, Van is the visionary of the family. As an ordained reverend, he has a way of communicating with people that is very rare. People feel comfortable with Van. When they come to him for his input, he's always willing to listen and to try and help that person out.

Even when Van was a little boy, he went out of his way trying to help and protect people. He used to get into a lot of fights because he could never just stand by and watch someone get bullied. He may have been a small boy, but he was tough and everyone in the neighborhood knew it. You just didn't mess with Van Woods. Nowadays, the only battles he gets into are the intellectual kind.

So whenever one of Van's friends comes around looking for him, he can count on his wife, Brenda, to quickly cook up a big batch of his favorite garlic chicken. Van absolutely loves garlic, and there's plenty of it here. Truth be told, Van isn't much of a cook, and since he lives near the restaurant, he really doesn't have to be. But when he and Brenda do cook, this is what they make. And it is delicious.

One 3 ½-pound chicken, cut into eighths

1 ½ teaspoons Sylvia's Secret Seasoning or dried herb mixture (page 81)

1 teaspoon salt

1 teaspoon freshly ground black pepper

¼ cup water

¼ cup chopped onion

¼ cup chopped green bell pepper

3 cloves garlic, minced

1. Preheat the oven to 350°F. Rinse the chicken and pat dry.

2. Stir together Sylvia's Secret Seasoning, salt, and pepper. Sprinkle all over the chicken pieces. Let stand for at least for 30 minutes or, even better, overnight in the refrigerator. Place into a 2-quart casserole. Add the water. Bake, uncovered, for 30 minutes, turning once or twice.

3. Combine the onion, bell pepper, and garlic. Sprinkle over the chicken. Return to the oven and bake for 30 minutes longer or until the chicken is cooked through.

If you can't find Sylvia's Secret Seasoning in your supermarket, you can use this blend instead.

DRIED HERB MIXTURE
Makes 1¾ tablespoons

1 tablespoon dried basil
1 teaspoon dried oregano
½ teaspoon dried thyme
¼ teaspoon dried rosemary, crumbled

In a medium bowl toss all the herbs to combine and use the quantity called for in the recipe.

The Absolute Best Southern Fried Chicken

Makes 4 servings

Julia Pressley

My mother, Julia, made some of the best fried chicken in all of South Carolina. She had her secrets to making it crunchy on the outside but keeping it tender on the inside. First of all, she would always shake the chicken in the coating, never dredge it. Then she cooked the chicken in a deep layer of oil in a black iron pan.

Fried chicken was a dish that she made for holidays, and oftentimes for Sunday dinner. She also fried up a batch before sending the children anywhere by train, since fried chicken makes the most delicious sandwiches imaginable. She would put the chicken between two slices of white bread, which were covered with mayonnaise. The longer the chicken sandwiches sat, the better they tasted, since the crumblings from the chicken skin and the mayonnaise would soak into the soft white bread. My son, Kenneth, would sometimes just eat the bread by itself before eating the chicken, since it tasted so good. The sandwiches were packed into a shoebox with some fruit and maybe a piece of cake or pie. You were supposed to wait until lunchtime to eat the chicken sandwiches, but none of the kids could ever wait that long. Kenny tells the story like this:

"I can remember those chicken sandwiches that my grandmother would pack for me to take on the train back to New York. It was a long train trip, maybe thirteen hours, and Grandma would make sure to pack me plenty of food. I could hardly wait to get on the train and eat those sandwiches because the aroma would just come out of the box and grab my attention. And my stomach would start rumbling and my mouth would start watering. Grandma would be waving good-bye, tears in her eyes, and I wouldn't really be paying attention. Almost before the train pulled off, I would have torn open the box and have wrapped my mouth around a fried chicken sandwich. Boy, they were great!"

One 3 ¹/₂-pound chicken, cut into eighths	¹/₂ teaspoon garlic powder
1 ¹/₂ teaspoons salt	¹/₂ cup all-purpose flour
1 ¹/₄ teaspoons freshly ground black pepper, divided	¹/₄ teaspoon paprika
	1 cup vegetable oil

1. Rinse the chicken and pat dry. In a small bowl, combine the salt, 1 teaspoon of the black pepper, and the garlic powder. Sprinkle over the chicken. Let stand at least 20 minutes or, even better, overnight in the refrigerator.

2. Place the flour, the remaining ¼ teaspoon black pepper, and paprika into a plastic bag. Add the seasoned chicken and shake until each piece is covered with the flour.

3. In a large skillet, heat the oil over high heat until it bubbles when a little flour is sprinkled in. Add the chicken pieces and reduce the heat to medium. Cook for 7 to 10 minutes or until the chicken is nicely browned on the bottom. Turn and cook on the other side for 7 to 10 minutes or until cooked through. Remove from the skillet and drain on paper towels before serving.

Modestine's Peachy Chicken

Makes 4 servings

Modestine Woodbury

Here's a recipe that my cousin Modestine makes for her family when the children come home from school to visit. It's an unusual combination of flavors and a dish that her whole family looks forward to. Modestine especially likes to serve it for Sunday dinner.

One 3 ½-pound chicken, cut into eighths

2 teaspoons lemon pepper seasoning

1 teaspoon salt

1 teaspoon freshly ground black pepper

One 16-ounce can sliced cling peaches in heavy syrup, undrained

1 tablespoon fresh lemon juice

1 tablespoon soy sauce

1. Preheat the oven to 350°F.

2. Rinse the chicken and pat dry; place in a 9 × 13 × 1¼-inch baking dish. In a small bowl, combine the lemon pepper, salt, and black pepper. Sprinkle both sides of the chicken pieces with the lemon pepper mixture; let stand for at least 20 minutes or, even better, overnight in the refrigerator.

3. Drain the syrup from the peaches into a small bowl. Stir the lemon juice and soy sauce into the syrup. Pour over the chicken pieces.

4. Bake for 1 hour, uncovered, turning once. Add the peach slices and bake for 15 minutes longer or until the chicken is cooked through.

Bedelia's Special Oven-Fried Chicken

Makes 4 servings

Bedelia Woods

I think Bedelia has developed quite a flair for cooking for diet-conscious eaters without sacrificing flavor. And these days, everyone in the family is concerned about their health. Don't think of traditional southern fried chicken when you think of this dish. It's something else entirely, and it is fabulous! Bedelia uses cornbread crumbs to coat the chicken instead of regular bread crumbs, and they make it very special. You can make this chicken for dinner, but it's also great for brunch, served with pancakes or waffles.

To get the crumbs, save any leftover cornbread in the freezer. When you want to make this recipe, defrost the cornbread and crumble it with a fork or in a blender or food processor. You can also use day-old cornbread for the crumbs. It works just as well.

Me, holding Bedelia, in 1949. We are sitting on our 1948 Buick, the car that took Herbert and me to California and back.

2 skinless and boneless breasts, halved (about 1 ½ pounds total)
1 tablespoon seasoned salt
1 teaspoon freshly ground black pepper
2 large egg whites
2 cups cornbread crumbs

1. Preheat the oven to 350°F. Rinse the chicken breasts and pat dry.

2. In a small bowl, combine the seasoned salt with the black pepper. Sprinkle over both sides of the chicken breasts. Let stand for at least 10 minutes.

3. In a bowl, beat the egg whites lightly. Dip the chicken breasts into the egg whites to coat. Dredge the chicken in the crumbs to coat. Place in a greased baking pan.

4. Bake for 35 to 40 minutes or until cooked through.

Bedelia's Dijon-Grilled Chicken

Makes 4 servings

Bedelia Woods

When my daughter Bedelia was a young girl, she decided that she wanted to cook me dinner on my birthday. Now, Bedelia was only twelve years old, but she chose a very challenging menu, including collard greens, candied yams with raisins and mushrooms, potato salad, and a whole roasted turkey.

The meal came out perfectly, except for one little problem. As she brought out the turkey, which was golden brown and just beautiful, she mentioned that it was different from other turkeys she had seen me and her grandma cook because there weren't any giblets in it.

Well, after we started to carve that bird, we found the giblets, still closed in their little bag. They were right inside the turkey. Let's just say that now Bedelia is an excellent cook.

2 skinless and boneless chicken breasts, halved (about 1 ½ pounds total)

2 tablespoons olive oil

2 teaspoons Sylvia's Secret Seasoning or dried herb mixture (page 81)

¼ cup Dijon mustard

2 tablespoons balsamic vinegar

1 tablespoon fresh lemon juice

2 cloves garlic, minced

1. Rinse the chicken breasts and pat dry. Between two pieces of waxed paper, pound the chicken breasts until ¼ inch thick. Brush each side of the chicken with the olive oil and sprinkle with Sylvia's Secret Seasoning; let stand for at least 10 minutes.

2. In a small bowl, stir together the mustard, vinegar, lemon juice, and garlic.

3. Cook the chicken breasts on a preheated grill or in a preheated broiler for 2 to 3 minutes per side or until almost cooked through. Brush each side with the mustard mixture and cook for 1 minute more per side.

On Bedelia's wedding day: me, Bedelia, and Julia (my mom).

Chicken and Rice Perlow | *Makes 4 to 6 servings*

Frances Donnelly

If you've never heard of rice perlow, it's because you haven't spent any time in Hemingway, South Carolina. Around there, rice perlows are served almost anytime a group of people get together—for holidays, picnics, cookouts, family reunions, funerals, and parties. The word comes from pilau, or pilaf, and the dish is always made from some combination of white rice and meat, chicken, or seafood.

You can also make perlow with small game birds, like my mother used to do. In fact, that's what she made for my son Kenneth the first time he went out hunting by himself.

"Every year," Kenneth reminisces when he tells this story, "my grandmother would burn the fields to recrop. And after they were burnt, the fields would fill with birds—blackbirds—who grazed there. This was the opportune time to hunt, because there would be hundreds and hundreds of blackbirds right by the house. So, my grandmother—I was about nine at the time—said, 'Well, I am going to let you shoot the shotgun for the first time by yourself, and if you kill enough birds, I will make you a bird perlow.' She told me to go out into the field, aim, and holler. And as soon as you make the noise, you pull the trigger. And I must have killed about twelve birds in that one shot. She made a bird perlow that evening and I was very proud to have brought home supper for everyone."

If you haven't just hunted for your dinner, you can make this fabulous recipe for chicken and rice perlow, which was given to me by my sister-in-law Frances Donnelly. It is one of her specialties, and we look forward to eating it every time the family gets together.

2 pounds chicken parts	1 tablespoon vegetable oil
1 ½ teaspoons Old Bay seasoning	2 slices bacon, cut into pieces
1 ½ teaspoons seasoned salt	¼ cup chopped onion
1 ½ teaspoons freshly ground black pepper	3 cups water
½ teaspoon salt	1 ½ cups converted white rice
½ teaspoon garlic salt	

1. Rinse the chicken and pat dry. Combine the Old Bay seasoning, seasoned salt, pepper, salt, and garlic salt. Sprinkle the chicken with the seasonings. Let stand for at least 2 hours or, even better, overnight in the refrigerator.

2. In a 6-quart Dutch oven, heat the oil over medium-high heat. Add the bacon and fry until cooked through but not crisp. Add the onion to the pot and cook, stirring, until softened, for about 2 minutes. Add the chicken and 1 cup of the water to the pot. Cook, uncovered, over medium heat for 45 minutes, stirring occasionally.

3. Remove the chicken from the pot and cut the chicken meat into smaller pieces (removing the bones and skin if desired).

4. Add the remaining 2 cups of water to the pot and bring to a boil. Reduce the heat and simmer, covered, for 15 minutes. Stir in the rice and cook, covered, for 15 minutes. Return the cut-up chicken to the pot and cook for 5 to 10 minutes longer or until the rice has absorbed the liquid and the chicken is heated.

"Herbal Chicken" | *Makes 4 servings*

Here's another chicken recipe designed for light eaters. Now, since Sylvia's is a soul food restaurant, we don't get too many customers planning on eating lightly. They come to us knowing what they want before they even step through the door, and if they are on a diet, they usually leave it in the car.

But this recipe tastes so delicious that it's become popular with all our customers, even the ones who usually eat their chicken fried and smothered. And if you are concerned about your health, you've got nothing to worry about here.

2 skinless, boneless chicken breast cutlets, halved (about 1 ½ pounds total)

1 tablespoon Old Bay seasoning

1 tablespoon dried parsley flakes

1 teaspoon Sylvia's Secret Seasoning or dried herb mixture (page 81)

1 tablespoon minced garlic

2 tablespoons vegetable oil

1. Rinse the chicken and pat dry. Cut the chicken cutlets in half to make eight pieces. In a small bowl, combine the Old Bay seasoning, parsley flakes, Sylvia's Secret Seasoning and garlic. Sprinkle over the chicken. Let stand for at least 20 minutes or, even better, overnight in the refrigerator.

2. Heat the oil in a large skillet. Cook the chicken over medium heat for about 7 minutes or until no longer pink in the middle, turning once.

Southern Fried Chicken Livers

Makes 4 servings

When I was growing up, we never bought chicken livers to fry. The chicken livers just came with the chickens that we slaughtered for Sunday dinner. When we fried the chicken, we naturally fried up the liver, too. Whoever liked the liver would take it. It was like any other part of the chicken, like the drumsticks or the wings. But now, it's more usual to make fried chicken livers as its own special dish. You can buy the livers separately in the supermarket, and fry them up with onions and peppers until they are golden brown and tender. But next time you fry a whole chicken, don't throw away the liver. Fry it up and eat it with your meal, just like we used to do.

2 pounds chicken livers

1 teaspoon salt

1 teaspoon freshly ground black pepper

³/₄ cup all-purpose flour

¹/₂ to ³/₄ cup vegetable oil

2 cups sliced onion

2 cups sliced green bell pepper

1. Thoroughly rinse the chicken livers and pat dry. Season with salt and pepper and let stand for at least 10 minutes or, even better, overnight in the refrigerator. Coat generously with flour.

2. In a large skillet, heat ½ cup of the oil over medium-high heat. Add the chicken livers and cook, turning once, until no longer pink in the center, for 5 to 7 minutes.

3. Remove the livers from the skillet. Add the onion and bell pepper (and more of the oil, if necessary). Cook, stirring, for 5 to 7 minutes or until the vegetables are tender. Serve the vegetables over the livers.

Sylvia's Special Roasted Turkey

Makes 8 to 10 servings

Although we take the whole family home to South Carolina for Christmas and Labor Day, we all spend Thanksgiving in New York. There's always a crowd coming over to our house, which is really like an open house, with everyone welcome. When we lived in the Bronx in a two-family house, with Bedelia and her family downstairs and Herbert, Crizette, and me upstairs, we would have so many people over for the holiday that we had to use every room of both apartments. All of our Connecticut relatives would come, my aunt Sarah and many of her thirteen children, plus their families. One year, we counted seventy-five people!

Everyone would cook and would bring things to eat. There were sweet potatoes, greens, peas and rice, turnips, potato salad, macaroni and cheese, venison, cakes, pies, and vanilla ice cream. And there was always my special roasted turkey. All the food was spread out on the dining-room table and in the kitchen, and everyone would take a plate and find a little corner to sit in. It was always such a treat to see the family. We had some people who would be so excited to come and visit that they would get to the house at ten-thirty in the morning and stay and help and eat all day long. Thanksgiving is real family time and a great excuse for spending time with one another. There's nothing I like better than that.

One 10- to 12-pound turkey
2 tablespoons Old Bay seasoning
1 tablespoon Sylvia's Secret Seasoning or
dried herb mixture (page 81)
$\frac{1}{2}$ teaspoon freshly ground black pepper

$\frac{1}{2}$ teaspoon garlic powder
$\frac{1}{4}$ cup ($\frac{1}{2}$ stick) butter
2 $\frac{1}{4}$ cups water, divided
6 tablespoons flour

1. Rinse the turkey and pat dry; remove the neck and innards.

2. In a small bowl, combine the Old Bay seasoning, Sylvia's Secret Seasoning, black pepper, and garlic powder. Sprinkle the seasonings all over the turkey, inside and out. Let stand for at least 1 hour or, even better, overnight in the refrigerator.

3. Preheat the oven to 350°F. Place the turkey, breast side down, in a roasting pan. Place the butter in the pan. Bake for 1 hour or until the back of the turkey is browned and crispy. Turn the turkey over; stir ¾ cup of the water into the pan and brush the turkey with the liquid from the pan. Roast for 1½ to 2 hours longer or until the thermometer reads 170°F when it is inserted in the thickest part of the breast (or until the plastic thermometer pops), and brush with pan drippings every 20 minutes or so.

4. Remove the turkey from the pan. In a bowl, stir together the flour and the remaining 1½ cups water. Stir into the roasting pan, scraping up all the browned bits from the bottom of the pan. Pour into a 1½-quart saucepan. Bring to a boil over medium-high heat, stirring constantly. Serve with the turkey.

Thanksgiving at our house in the Bronx, about 1981.

Sweet and Sour Sassy Turkey Wings

Makes 4 servings

Vanessa Hill

This is the kind of recipe that is perfect to serve to a crowd of hungry relatives and friends. My cousin Vanessa says that she likes to make it for birthday parties and graduations, but really they're great anytime. The sauce for the wings is what makes them really special. It's sweet from the crushed pineapple and apricot preserves, sour from the vinegar, and sassy from the barbecue sauce.

Bedelia and my cousin Vanessa in the kitchen of our house in the Bronx on Thanksgiving, about 1981.

8 turkey wings, tips and first joint only (4 pounds)

2 teaspoons salt

2 teaspoons freshly ground black pepper

1 teaspoon poultry seasoning

1 ½ cups chopped onion

1 ½ cups chopped green bell pepper

1 cup chopped celery

2 cloves garlic, minced

Two 8-ounce cans crushed pineapple in juice

½ cup apricot preserves

½ cup firmly packed dark brown sugar

½ cup barbecue sauce

¼ cup cider vinegar

1. Preheat the oven to 350°F.

2. Wash and pat dry and disjoint the turkey wings.

3. In a small bowl, combine the salt, pepper, and poultry seasoning. Sprinkle over the turkey wings. Let stand at least 20 minutes or, even better, overnight in the refrigerator. Place the turkey wings in a 6-quart Dutch oven and sprinkle with the onion, green pepper, celery, and garlic. Cover and bake for 3 hours or until tender. Remove the wings from the pot (leave the juices from baking in the pot). Place the wings in a large roasting pan and set aside.

4. Add the pineapple with the juice, apricot preserves, brown sugar, barbecue sauce, and vinegar to the pot with the juices from baking. Bring to a boil on top of the stove. Pour over the turkey wings in the roasting pan. Return to the oven and bake for 30 minutes, turning once.

Tender Stewed Chicken Gizzards

Makes 4 servings

Mattie McFadden

Like chicken livers, chicken gizzards were never bought by themselves. They were something extra that you got when you killed your chickens for Sunday. Usually, you wouldn't stew the gizzards by themselves because there really weren't enough of them to bother. Instead, we used to use the gizzards, along with the necks and the feet, to make gravy. We would put everything in a pot with some water and boil it until it got to be a really flavorful broth. Then we would use it to make gravy. We always saved the gizzards from the broth because they were so good to eat. All the children loved them and everyone got a little taste.

With this recipe, which is from my daughter-in-law Brenda's mother, there are finally enough gizzards to go around, and they cook up deliciously tender and flavorful. You can buy chicken gizzards at the supermarket. Or, whenever you use a whole chicken, save the gizzards in the freezer until you have enough to make this dish.

1 ½ pounds chicken gizzards

1 teaspoon salt

1 teaspoon freshly ground black pepper

2 cups water

¾ cup chopped onion

1 tablespoon ketchup

1 teaspoon hot sauce

Cooked rice

1. Sprinkle the gizzards with the salt and pepper; let stand for 10 minutes or, even better, overnight in the refrigerator.

2. In a 3-quart saucepan, bring the water to a boil; add the gizzards, reduce the heat and simmer, covered, for 30 minutes. Add the onion, ketchup, and hot sauce and simmer for 1 hour longer, uncovered.

3. Serve over rice.

Beef

Of all the animals on our farm, only two types were named like pets: the mules and the cows. Herbert remembers the name of one of his mules, Jack, and I can remember a few of the cows—Merry, Sue, Red, and Belle. They all grazed in the fields around our house. You chained them in one area for a few days, and when they had grazed it clean, you would move them to another area until the first one grew back. Cows make great lawn mowers.

Mostly, the cows were pretty tame, except when one of them was pregnant. Then, if you tried to go out in the fields and bother one of them, like my son Kenneth did one time, they would come after you. Poor Kenneth was annoying Merry when she was expecting, and she ran him all the way down the lane into a neighbor's house. Kenneth swears he felt those cow horns digging into his behind as he ran up the stairs of his cousin McGill's back porch. I think he was exaggerating, but still, it's scary being chased by an angry cow.

Since cows grazed on their own for their food, you didn't have to feed them every day. But you did have to milk them every day. Some people are good at milking cows and some just aren't. I was pretty good at it, and when I went over to Merry or Belle with my milking pail and stool, they'd move their legs aside, letting me underneath to take hold of the udder.

Milking cows was fun for a chore. You'd work the cow's teats, one in each hand, and pull just right, moving your thumbs up and down. If the cow didn't like you, or if you weren't pulling right, nothing would come out. If you hurt her, the cow would knock over your pail of milk with a quick kick or swat you in the face with her tail. If you wanted to, you could make music while milking. You pulled those teats to a beat and listened while the milk hit the tin pail: squish squish squish squish squish squish squish.

You could get about a gallon of milk with each milking, which came halfway up the pail. Then we strained it and put it in the safe overnight, or later in the refrigerator. In the morning the milk would have separated with the cream on top and the milk on the bottom. The cream was skimmed off the top and put into a jar, waiting to be churned into butter. And the milk was drunk with breakfast, or made into pudding or cake.

So our cows were much more important than just for beef. But they were good for that, too. Slaughtering time, like for the hogs, was in the winter. Beef was eaten either fresh or frozen; you didn't really cure it where I came from. Before we got our freezer, we kept the meat in town in a public icebox, where you could rent a cold little cubby to store your supply. Once we got our freezer, though, we just kept it in there. This way, we could enjoy our favorite beef dishes all year long, without even leaving the house.

Tender Pot Roast | *Makes 6 to 8 servings*

Mary M. Brown

After church on Sunday, all the family used to gather at my mother's house to share Sunday dinner. The meal began around two in the afternoon and would last for at least two or three hours. People would visit together, and it was a time for the family to really talk.

Now, my mother's Sunday dinner was a huge meal. You see, where I come from, most Southerners try to serve two meats on Sundays. You would always have a chicken—in the South there's a chicken in every pot on Sundays—and you could have either beef or pork. Pot-roasted beef was a favorite dish to serve in the winter. Although it never got that cold in South Carolina, don't forget that we also didn't have a chimney in every room. So we needed hearty food to keep us warm. For this, there is nothing better than a steaming dish of tender pot roast, cooked with carrots and onions like this recipe from our friend Mary M. Brown. She says that this dish has been her daughter's favorite for years. One bite and you'll know why.

One 3- to 4-pound chuck or rump roast

2 cups peeled carrot chunks (1-inch pieces)

2 cups peeled potato chunks (1-inch pieces)

2 small yellow onions, peeled and cut into quarters

One 10 ¹/₂-ounce can golden mushroom soup

1 package dried onion soup mix

¹/₂ cup water

¹/₂ teaspoon freshly ground black pepper

1. Preheat the oven to 300°F.

2. Place the roast in a 6-quart Dutch oven. Surround the roast with the carrot and potato chunks and onions. In a medium bowl, stir together the mushroom soup, onion soup mix, water, and pepper. Pour over the roast and vegetables. Cover tightly with aluminum foil.

3. Bake for 4 to 5 hours or until tender.

4. Let stand for 10 minutes, then slice the roast and serve surrounded by the vegetables. Serve the gravy on the side.

Frances's Minute Steak with Gravy

Makes 4 servings

Frances Donnelly

My sister-in-law Frances is an excellent cook. She learned at an early age from her mother, who, after her father died, worked as a housekeeper for another family nearby. Since her mother was always working, she taught Frances how to cook for the three younger children. Frances and her mother worked hard to bring the younger ones up right, and it worked because all four children, Frances included, went to college when they grew up.

This is Frances's recipe for minute steak. The nice thing about it is how quick it makes both a delicious steak dinner and the gravy that goes with it. Frances serves it over rice to sop up all that good pan gravy.

1 teaspoon garlic salt

½ teaspoon salt

½ teaspoon freshly ground black pepper

½ teaspoon Old Bay seasoning

1 pound minute steak (4 to 5 medium pieces)

⅓ cup self-rising flour

6 tablespoons butter or margarine

1 medium onion, sliced

1 cup warm water

1. Preheat the oven to 400°F.

2. Combine the garlic salt, salt, pepper, and Old Bay seasoning. Sprinkle the seasonings evenly over both sides of the steaks. Let stand for 20 minutes. Dust the steaks with the flour.

3. Melt the butter in a large skillet over medium-high heat. Add the steaks and brown lightly on both sides, 2 to 3 minutes per side. Place into a 1½-quart casserole dish. Sprinkle the onion slices over the meat.

4. Add any remaining flour to the skillet that the meat was cooked in. Stir until the flour is absorbed. Add the water and cook over high heat, stirring up the browned bits from the bottom of the pan. Bring to a boil, then reduce the heat and simmer for 1 minute. Pour over the steaks. Cover and bake for 35 minutes or until the meat is tender.

Frances and Robert Donnelly (Herbert's brother and sister-in-law) and their children.

Southern-Style Beef Stew | *Makes 4 to 6 servings*

We raised our own cows in Hemingway when I was a girl, and because of this, we ate a lot of beef when we slaughtered one of them. Naturally we would have plenty of meat, and so would all our neighbors within walking distance. Cows were usually slaughtered in November and December before Christmas. You would kill the cow in the winter, since, back before we had refrigeration, the meat would keep longer in cold weather.

My mother would have the cow slaughtered and the beef cut up into steaks, roasts, and ribs, ground into hamburger, and cubed for stewing. This beef stew was one of our favorite dishes to serve for Sunday dinner. We would generally serve it with rice, but mashed potatoes, macaroni and cheese, or candied yams are good with it, too.

2 tablespoons vegetable oil

3 pounds cubed stewing beef (chuck or neck)

5 cups water

One 16-ounce can stewed tomatoes

2 cups carrot pieces (1 1/2 inches long)

1 cup chopped celery

1 cup chopped onion

1 teaspoon lemon pepper seasoning

3 cups cubed potatoes (1-inch cubes)

1 cup chopped green bell pepper

1 teaspoon salt

1/4 teaspoon freshly ground black pepper

1. In a 6-quart Dutch oven, heat the oil over medium-high heat. Add the beef and cook, stirring, until nicely browned on all sides, for about 6 minutes. Add the water, tomatoes, carrot, celery, onion, and lemon pepper seasoning. Bring to a boil. Reduce the heat and simmer for 1½ hours, uncovered.

2. Add the potatoes, green pepper, salt, and black pepper. Return to a boil. Reduce the heat and simmer, uncovered, for 20 to 30 minutes longer, or until the potatoes are tender.

Chili from the A&J | *Makes 3 to 4 servings*

Camellia Chinnes Lane

When I was growing up, the A&J was the only real restaurant in Hemingway. It was located in the bus station, right in the center of town. When I reached the daughter of one of the owners, Camellia Chinnes Lane, and told her about our cookbook, she immediately sent in the recipe for the chili that they used to serve over their hamburger steaks and in sloppy Joes. It was famous in its day, and when you make it, you'll see why.

1 pound ground beef

1 cup chopped onion

2 tablespoons chili powder

1/2 teaspoon salt

1/2 teaspoon freshly ground black pepper

1 1/2 cups canned tomato sauce

1/2 cup water

1. In a large skillet over medium-high heat, cook the ground beef with the onion until the beef is no longer pink, about 4 minutes. Drain off all excess fat.

2. Return the skillet to the heat and stir in the chili powder, salt, and black pepper until absorbed. Stir in the tomato sauce and water. Bring to a boil, reduce the heat, and simmer for 10 to 15 minutes or until thickened.

3. Serve as a topper for hot dogs or hamburgers or as chili.

Barbecued Beef Short Ribs

Makes 4 servings

Bedelia Woods

My eldest daughter, Bedelia, is known for being quite a cook. Whenever the family gets together for a holiday or a picnic, you'll find Bedelia in the kitchen, cooking up some of her delicious recipes to share with everyone. I think she takes after me in this way—wanting to feed and take care of people. When we all lived in the Bronx in a two-family house, with Bedelia and her family downstairs and the rest of my family upstairs, the youngest children knew that if they wanted a snack, they could go and look in Bedelia's kitchen; she liked to keep her homemade goodies around for the taking. And believe me, those kids appreciated it.

One thing that Bedelia loves to make for any occasion is her barbecued short ribs. Bedelia is just crazy about barbecue—she'll barbecue anything she gets her hands on, including shrimp, chicken, fish, beef, or pigs' feet. She even adds barbecue sauce to her Sassy Rice (page 202)! This barbecue recipe is really perfect to serve for a crowd when your own family and friends get together. I know they'll enjoy it as much as we do.

3 ½ to 4 pounds short ribs of beef (flanken)

1 teaspoon salt

1 teaspoon freshly ground black pepper

1 teaspoon crushed red pepper flakes

¾ cup chopped onion

½ cup chopped celery

½ cup chopped green bell pepper

2 cloves garlic, minced

1 ½ cups barbecue sauce

1 tablespoon steak sauce

1. Preheat the oven to 350°F.

2. Cut the strips of short ribs, between each bone, into pieces. In a small bowl, combine the salt, black pepper, and red pepper flakes. Sprinkle all over the pieces of beef. Place in a 9 × 13 × 2-inch baking pan. Sprinkle with the onion, celery, bell pepper, and garlic.

3. Bake, covered with aluminum foil, for 1½ hours.

4. In a bowl, stir together the barbecue sauce and steak sauce. Pour over the ribs and bake for 1½ hours longer or until the meat is tender when pierced with a fork, turning the ribs every half hour.

Bedelia in front of the smokehouse, about 1959.

Wednesday Night Special Meat Loaf

Makes 4 to 6 servings

Meat loaf is our Wednesday night special at the restaurant. When my younger daughter, Crizette, was still a child, I would bring it home to her every week, with a side of mashed potatoes and greens.

This recipe gains its unique Southern flavor from the barbecue sauce I use with the beef. The sauce makes the meat loaf extra sassy and extra delicious. Make sure you use a soft white bread here; you don't want any hard crusts interfering with the meat.

3 slices white bread

2 pounds ground beef

³/₄ cup chopped onion

¹/₂ cup chopped celery

¹/₃ cup chopped green bell pepper

2 large eggs

1 cup tomato puree

³/₄ cup barbecue sauce, divided

1 teaspoon salt

1 teaspoon hot pepper sauce

¹/₂ teaspoon seasoned salt

1 tablespoon light or dark brown sugar

1. Preheat the oven to 350°F.

2. Place the bread into a blender or food processor and process into coarse crumbs.

3. In a large bowl, combine the beef, onion, celery, green pepper, eggs, and bread crumbs. In a medium bowl, combine the tomato puree, ½ cup barbecue sauce, salt, hot pepper sauce, and seasoned salt. Pour into the meat mixture and combine with your hands.

4. Form into a loaf and place into a 9 × 5 × 3-inch loaf pan.

5. Stir the brown sugar into the reserved ¼ cup barbecue sauce. Pour over the loaf. Bake for 1 hour or until cooked through.

Black Bean and Oxtail Stew

Makes 4 servings

I am just crazy about oxtails; they're so meaty and rich tasting. I make them at the restaurant, and believe me, I have turned around a number of people who thought they wouldn't like them! Cooking oxtails with black beans and sausage makes a filling dish just right for a cold winter supper. I serve it with rice and collard greens.

1 cup dried black beans

Water

1 pound sage sausage, breakfast sausage, or Italian sweet sausage

2 tablespoons vegetable oil

1 pound oxtails

1 teaspoon poultry seasoning

1 teaspoon salt

¹/₂ teaspoon ground red pepper

¹/₂ teaspoon Goya adobo all-purpose seasoning

1. In a large bowl, cover the beans with water and let stand overnight; drain.

2. In a 6-quart pot, cook the sausage in boiling water to cover for 10 minutes; drain.

3. Add the oil to the pot and heat over medium-high heat. Add the oxtails to the pot. Cook until browned all over, about 6 minutes.

4. Add 4 cups fresh water and the beans to the pot. Bring to a boil, reduce the heat and simmer, uncovered, for 1 to 1½ hours or until the beans are almost tender. Stir in the sausage and the seasonings and simmer for 30 minutes longer.

Pork

Can you imagine everyone in the same community going to the same barbecue place to get their hog cooked for Christmas? Well, that's exactly what happens every year in Hemingway.

My mother used to have a special galvanized metal tub which she would use to haul the hog that we were going to barbecue down the road to Clarence and Henry's barbecue. They were my mother's cousins. You had to plan to barbecue the hog at least a week in advance, so you'd have the time to get it slaughtered. Clarence and Henry could cook at least eight hogs at a time, and they would have them all lined up on a long metal grill over the fire.

Now, the pigs that my mother sent to be barbecued were the pigs that we raised on the farm. Kids today don't really understand where their food comes from, but we knew exactly where ours did—from our own backyard, mostly.

Feeding the pigs was a bigger chore than feeding the chickens because the slop pail was so heavy. That's what people fed their hogs back then, leftovers from the kitchen. Anytime you peeled your potatoes or trimmed your greens, you put the waste in the slop pail. We also fed the hogs the water we cooked potatoes or macaroni in, and leftover bread and hominy grits. We hardly wasted a thing, back in the day.

Anyway, we slopped the pigs twice a day, once in the morning and once in the afternoon. The slop pail was hard to carry, especially if you were a child, and usually it's the children who have to slop the pigs. The little ones who couldn't manage the pail themselves would slide it onto a tobacco stick, which two of them would carry together, one on each end. Once the hogs saw you coming with their breakfast, they would run over to the trough and stand there, waiting for you.

November was when we started slaughtering the hogs. The meat would last longer in cooler weather. After butchering the hogs, we made our own hams and sausages. First, you would start preparing the hams. You'd pat a thick layer of salt onto the pork shoulders, then wrap a wire around them and hang them in the smoke-house. After that, every six days you'd take the hams down and salt them again. It took about one and a half days for every pound of ham to cure, so a twenty-pound ham took thirty days.

You'd make your sausages out of the trimmings from the hams, which you ground up real fine with any other hog trimmings you'd have on hand. Then you'd season it with salt, pepper, and whatever other seasoning you liked. My grandmother used a mix of crushed red pepper and plenty of sage for her sausages. The best part about making sausages was stuffing the pork mixture into the casings. Hog intestines were *used back then and I think they probably still are. At the end of the meat grinder was a long, thin funnel attachment. You placed the sausage casing on one end and forced the meat into it through the funnel by turning the handle on the grinder. All the kids loved to stuff the sausages. Then those were hung up in the smokehouse with the hams, and we ate them all winter long.*

Me and Van in 1973 at a Jeremiah Church fund-raiser and fashion show.

Chopped Barbecued Pork | *Makes 6 to 8 servings*

Barbecued pork was a dish that was served on holidays and especially on Thanksgiving and Christmas. It used to be that all the men got together on Christmas Eve and barbecued a whole hog for Christmas dinner the next day. First, they dug a hole in the ground. Over the hole they put up some bricks or stone and put a wire grate on top. The charcoal went into the hole underneath the grate, and the hog went over the grate. You'd have to cook the hog real slow, otherwise the fat on the outside would burn before the inside was cooked, so it took maybe seven or eight hours. And the men would sit outside with the hog, watching it cook, talking, and laughing, and maybe taking little sips of holiday cheer while they waited.

Well, one year Herbert was out there with his friends, doing the barbecue and having little sips all through the night. When Christmas came, at midnight, the pig was finished, but Herbert didn't take it off the fire. Instead, since it was Christmas, he wanted to come inside the house and give me a merry Christmas kiss. He walked over to kiss me and as he started to give me a hug, he looked out of the window. "Oh, my God," he said, "the hog is burning up!" The hog fat caught fire and spread so fast that the whole house almost went up. That was the last time Herbert ever barbecued a whole hog.

But we still make this easy recipe for chopped barbecued pork. You cook only the shoulder, and you can do it in the safety of your own kitchen—no barbecue pit needed! You can use other cuts of pork, not just the shoulder. Try pork butt or ham (uncooked).

One 6- to 7-pound fresh shoulder of pork	**¹⁄₂ cup water**
1 teaspoon paprika	**¹⁄₂ cup cider vinegar**
1 teaspoon salt	**¹⁄₂ cup minced onion**
1 teaspoon freshly ground black pepper	**¹⁄₄ cup firmly packed dark or light brown**
1 cup chopped onion	**sugar**
	1 teaspoon chili powder
FOR THE BARBECUE SAUCE	**1 teaspoon salt**
1 cup sweetened applesauce	**1 teaspoon freshly ground black pepper**
¹⁄₂ cup ketchup	

1. Preheat the oven to 350°F.

2. Season the pork shoulder with the paprika, salt, and pepper. Bake in a 9 × 13 × ½-inch baking pan for 2 to 3 hours or until very tender. Remove from the oven and cool. Remove the meat from the bones and chop. Add the chopped onion to the chopped pork shoulder.

3. While the pork is roasting in a 1-quart saucepan, combine all of the barbecue sauce ingredients. Bring to a boil over high heat. Reduce the heat and simmer for 1 hour.

4. Return the chopped pork and onion to a 9 × 13-inch baking pan and pour the sauce over it. Bake for 30 minutes.

My mother and her cousin Sylvia Smith on Labor Day, 1973. Mama is holding an award we gave her for being the best mother of the year.

Daughter-in-Law Sylvia's Barbecued Pork Chops

Makes 4 to 6 servings

Sylvia Brown Woods

Maybe I got it from my mother, but for some reason I always knew how to save money. Mama used to say, if you don't save a penny, you will never have a nickel. I always remember that. So, when I was a young lady, just after Herbert and I married and moved to New York, I was very careful about spending. One way to save money was to bring my lunch to work every day. At that time, I was working at a dye factory in New Jersey, and each morning, just like my mother did when she worked in New York, I packed my lunch. Usually, I would just take a little bit of whatever was left over from dinner the night before. Whatever it was went in between two slices of bread and you had a sandwich. I'd wrap the sandwich in waxed paper—you didn't have foil back then—and pack it with some fruit in a little brown bag. One of my favorite things to pack was leftover pork chops. And one of my favorite ways to eat pork chops is to barbecue them.

Here's a fantastic recipe for barbecued pork chops that Sylvia, my lovely daughter-in-law, makes. They are one of the reasons that my son Kenneth fell in love with her. You see, every time he would go over to her house for dinner when they were dating, she'd make barbecued pork chops for him. And now, even though they've been married for years, Sylvia still makes this dish for Kenneth. There's nothing he likes better.

6 pork chops (1/2 inch thick)	1 teaspoon steak sauce
1 teaspoon salt	1 cup barbecue sauce
1 teaspoon freshly ground black pepper	2 tablespoons sugar
1/2 cup chopped onion	1 teaspoon hot pepper sauce
1/4 cup water	

1. Preheat the oven to 350°F.

2. Rinse the pork chops and pat dry. Season with the salt and pepper; let stand for 20 minutes or, even better, overnight in the refrigerator.

3. Place the pork chops in a 9 × 13 × 1½-inch baking pan. Sprinkle with the onion. In a small bowl, stir together the water and steak sauce. Pour over the chops. Bake for 1 hour, covered.

4. In a medium bowl, combine 2 tablespoons of the pan drippings (discarding any extra), the barbecue sauce, sugar, and hot sauce. Pour over the chops, turning the chops to coat in the sauce. Bake, uncovered, for 10 minutes, turn the chops, and bake for 5 minutes longer.

Marinated Pork Roast | *Makes 4 to 6 servings*

Allie Christine "Tennie" Cameron

My cousin Tennie is known for her creative recipes, and this is definitely one of them. Who else in our family would have thought to marinate a pork roast in ginger ale and soy sauce? But it works and makes a different, delicious Sunday dinner. Tennie serves the roast with all the usual Sunday fixings—cornbread, collard greens, macaroni and cheese, and rice. There's nothing better.

One 12-ounce can ginger ale

1 ½ tablespoons soy sauce

1 tablespoon minced green bell pepper

1 teaspoon fresh lemon juice

1 teaspoon sugar

1 clove garlic, minced

1 bone-in center-cut pork roast (about 4 pounds)

2 tablespoons water

1 ½ tablespoons all-purpose flour

1. In a heavy resealable plastic bag or a 9-inch-square glass baking dish, combine the ginger ale, soy sauce, green pepper, lemon juice, sugar, and garlic. Add the pork roast and refrigerate overnight, turning once if possible.

2. Preheat the oven to 325°F.

3. Place the roast and marinade in a baking dish (if using the plastic bag) and bake for 1 hour and 45 minutes or until a thermometer reads 160° to 170°F.

4. Pour the juices from the pan into a 1-quart saucepan. In a small bowl, stir together the water and flour. Stir into the pan with the pan juices. Bring to a boil over medium-high heat. Serve with the roast.

PREVIOUS PAGE: *Beef Vegetable Soup
(page 70) with Frances's "You Can't
Eat Just One" Snackin' Crackers (page
72)*

ABOVE: *Bedelia's Barbecued Beef
Short Ribs (page 104), Sylvia's Collard
Greens with Smoked Turkey (page 187),
Bedelia's Sassy Rice (page 202), and
Sylvia's Steamin' Cornbread (page 217)*

LEFT: *Smothered Pork Chops
(page 117), with Garlic and
Herb Mashed Potatoes (page 175), and
Crizette's Garlic Fried Okra (page 184)*

BELOW: *Sallie Brown's Beautiful
Glazed Ham (page 121), Candy Yams
Soufflé (page 180), and Frances's Lily
White Biscuits (page 213)*

OPPOSITE. *Picnic Day:
Bedelia's Special Oven-
Fried Chicken (page 85),
Colorful Corn Salad
(page 172), Black-Eyed Pea
Salad (page 171), Crackling
Cornbread (page 218)*

ABOVE: *McKinley Preston's
Crispy Roast Duck with
Apple and Raisin Sauce
(page 143)*

TOP LEFT: *Felix and Sparkle's Crab and Corn Boil (page 162)*

BOTTOM LEFT: *My Mom Julia's Holiday Breakfast: Fried Fish (page 148), grits, Stewed Tomatoes and Okra (page 183), and Frances's Lily White Biscuits (page 213) with syrup*

ABOVE: *Herbert's Rise and Shine Salmon and Bacon with Grits (page 156), with fresh fruit*

OPPOSITE: *Tennie's Seriously Spicy Shrimp Stew (page 161)*

ABOVE: *Sallie's Luscious Lemony Pound Cake (page 248)*

LEFT: *Mary's Red Velvet Cake (page 258)*

Smothered Pork Chops | *Makes 2 to 4 servings*

This satisfying dish is perfect to serve when everybody is tired of chicken. It has plenty of flavor and is practically a meal in itself, since the pork chops make their own rich brown gravy with onion as they cook. You can eat the gravy over rice.

1 1/2 teaspoons salt, divided

1 teaspoon ground black pepper

1 teaspoon Sylvia's Secret Seasoning or dried herb mixture (page 81)

2 teaspoons garlic powder

Four 1-inch-thick loin pork chops (bone in)

1/2 cup all-purpose flour

1/2 cup vegetable oil

1/2 cup sliced onion

1/2 cup sliced green bell pepper

1 1/2 cups water

1. In a small bowl, combine the salt, black pepper, Sylvia's Secret Seasoning, and garlic powder. Sprinkle over both sides of the pork chops. Let stand for at least 20 minutes or, even better, overnight in the refrigerator.

2. Place the flour onto a piece of waxed paper. Dredge the pork chops in the flour until well coated (save any leftover flour for the gravy).

3. Heat the oil in a large skillet over high heat. Add the pork chops and cook for 6 to 8 minutes or until browned on the bottom. Turn and cook for 6 to 8 minutes or until browned on the other side. Remove the chops from the pan.

4. Pour off two-thirds of the oil. Add the onion and green pepper and cook, stirring, until the onion is transparent, for about 2 minutes. Add 2 tablespoons of the flour from the dredging (if there isn't enough, add extra flour to equal 2 tablespoons). Stir in the water until smooth. Return the chops to the pan. Bring to a boil. Cover the pan, reduce the heat, and simmer for 45 minutes.

Frances's Fabulous Spareribs

Makes 4 servings

Frances Donnelly

My sister-in-law Frances is one of the most caring, most mothering, and kindest people I know. She hardly ever thinks of herself, and is always looking for ways to make people happy. Let me tell you a little story so you know what I mean: When we were at the cook-off at Jeremiah Church in Hemingway, people arrived at different times, so there was always a crowd. I saw Frances earlier in the day when she brought over her wonderful dishes, but then when I looked for her again, she wasn't there.

"Where's Frances?" I asked.

"Oh, Frances just left," someone told me, "but she'll be right back."

Well, Frances was afraid that there wasn't going to be enough to feed everybody, so she went home, then came back with pots and pots of more food. She had chicken and rice perlow, beans, and these excellent ribs. Even though there turned out to be plenty of food, these ribs seemed to be one of the first dishes to disappear. Try them and you'll see why.

4 to 5 pounds spareribs	$^2/_3$ cup Cane Patch syrup or Alagra syrup
1 teaspoon salt	(see Note) or dark brown sugar
$^1/_2$ teaspoon freshly ground black pepper	$^1/_3$ cup chopped onion
1 $^1/_4$ cups apple cider vinegar	$^1/_3$ cup chopped green bell pepper
1 cup ketchup	1 tablespoon fresh lemon juice
1 cup barbecue sauce	1 teaspoon crushed red pepper flakes

1. Separate the ribs into individual pieces. In a 6-quart pot, cover the ribs with water. Add the salt and pepper. Bring to a boil over high heat. Reduce the heat and simmer, uncovered, for 40 minutes.

2. While the ribs are cooking, prepare the sauce by combining the vinegar, ketchup, barbecue sauce, syrup, onion, bell pepper, lemon juice, and red pepper flakes in a 1½-quart saucepan. Bring to a boil over high heat. Reduce the heat and simmer, uncovered, for 10 minutes. Remove from the heat.

3. Preheat the oven to 400°F.

4. Drain the ribs and place on a 10 × 15-inch baking (jelly-roll) pan. Pour the sauce over the ribs and turn to coat the ribs. Bake for 20 minutes, covered with aluminum foil. Turn the ribs and bake, uncovered, for 20 minutes longer.

NOTE: If you can't find Cane Patch or Alagra syrup, try substituting Karo dark corn syrup or even pancake syrup with a little molasses added for flavor. You want the flavor of molasses, but straight molasses is much too strong.

Nan's Extra-Special Marinated Spareribs

Makes 4 to 6 servings

Nan Puryear

There is so much I could say about our dear friend Nan and her wonderful spareribs. She is a one-of-a-kind spirit and makes one-of-a-kind ribs! The pineapple and the sherry in the barbecue sauce make them unusually delicious. They're just the thing when you need to serve a crowd of people. Believe me, they will disappear.

1 pound 4 ¹/₂-ounce can juice-packed pineapple chunks, drained and juice saved

¹/₃ cup soy sauce

¹/₄ cup ketchup

3 tablespoons cider vinegar

2 tablespoons sherry

2 tablespoons light or dark brown sugar

2 tablespoons minced fresh ginger or ground ginger

1 clove garlic, crushed

4 pounds baby back ribs

¹/₂ teaspoon salt

1 cup water

1. In a large bowl, combine ¼ cup of the pineapple juice, the soy sauce, ketchup, vinegar, sherry, brown sugar, ginger, and garlic. Add the ribs to the bowl and let marinate for at least 6 hours, or, even better, overnight in the refrigerator. Drain the ribs, reserving the marinade.

2. Preheat the oven to 325°F.

3. Sprinkle the ribs with the salt. Place the ribs on a rack in a jelly-roll pan containing the water. Bake for 45 minutes, turning once. Discard the drippings. Place the ribs in the pan (not on the rack) and pour on the reserved marinade. Bake for 30 minutes, turning the ribs once. Add the pineapple chunks and remaining pineapple juice. Bake for 30 minutes longer, turning the ribs once. Turn the ribs in the marinade one last time before serving.

Sallie Brown's Beautiful Glazed Ham

Makes 16 to 20 servings

Sallie Brown

Sallie Brown is a neighbor of ours in Hemingway, and she's also my son Kenneth's mother-in-law. Cooking is one of her favorite pastimes, ever since she was a little girl, when she would prepare meals for the family while her mother was working in the fields.

This recipe for glazed ham is one of Sallie's specialties. She likes to serve it for the holidays, especially for Christmas, when she decorates the platter with holly.

When I asked Sallie's daughter Doretha what her mother did with any leftovers, she laughed because there never were any. You see, her mother always made sure that everyone who came to dinner, even if she fed one hundred as she did sometimes, got a care package to take home. Gestures like these give Hemingway its reputation for Southern hospitality.

One 8- to 10-pound smoked ham

Water

FOR THE GLAZE
2 tablespoons vegetable oil
2 tablespoons minced onion
1 cup ketchup
½ cup water
3 tablespoons honey
2 tablespoons cider vinegar
1 tablespoon Worcestershire sauce
1 teaspoon hot pepper sauce

1. Place the ham in a 16-quart saucepan and add enough water to cover by 2 inches. Bring to a boil over medium-high heat. Reduce the heat and simmer, uncovered, for 1 hour; drain.

2. To make the glaze, in a 1-quart saucepan, heat the oil over medium-high heat. Add the onion and cook, stirring, for 1 minute or until softened. Remove from the heat. Stir in the ketchup, water, honey, vinegar, Worcestershire sauce, and hot pepper sauce.

3. Preheat the oven to 350°F.

4. Place the ham in a roasting pan. Pour the sauce over the ham. Bake for 30 minutes, basting occasionally. Slice and serve with the sauce from the pan on the side.

Modestine's Sausage and Grits Pie

Makes 4 to 6 servings as a main dish or 8 servings as a side dish

Modestine Woodbury

My cousin Modestine has done it again and come up with another creative recipe. Grits and sausage are two breakfast favorites in the South, but they are usually served separately. Here the grits and sausage are mixed with eggs and baked. Now all you need are the biscuits.

12 ounces breakfast sausage

4 ounces grated mild Cheddar cheese

½ teaspoon salt

1 ½ cups cooked grits

4 large eggs, beaten

1. Preheat the oven to 325°F. Grease a 9-inch pie dish.

2. Remove the sausage from its casing. Cook the sausage in a large skillet, over medium-high heat, until no longer pink, for about 5 minutes. Remove the skillet from the heat.

3. Stir the cheese and salt into the skillet, until the cheese is melted. Stir in the grits and the eggs.

4. Spoon the entire mixture into the pie dish. Bake for 45 minutes or until puffy and cooked through.

Baked Ham Supreme

Makes 12 to 16 servings

Vanessa Hill

My cousin Vanessa's recipe for baked ham is sweet and spicy—just like Vanessa herself. I know you'll love it just as much as our family does. If you have any leftovers, don't heat them up; make baked-ham sandwiches instead. There's nothing better.

One 8-pound smoked ham (butt half)
One 32-ounce can pineapple juice
Whole cloves
One 16-ounce bottle A-1 steak sauce
One 8-ounce bottle honey

1. Trim off the excess fat from the ham. Place the ham in a nonreactive baking dish. Pour the pineapple juice over the ham and let marinate in the refrigerator overnight, turning the ham occasionally. Remove the ham from the dish and reserve half of the pineapple juice.

2. Preheat the oven to 400°F.

3. Score the ham decoratively and stud with cloves. Place the ham in a roasting pan with the reserved pineapple juice. Bake 2 hours, covered, basting occasionally.

4. While the ham is baking, in a medium bowl, stir together the A-1 sauce and honey. Discard any liquid from the roasting pan. Pour sauce over ham and bake for 20 minutes, basting once or twice.

White Bean and Sausage Stew

Makes 4 servings

Roberta Adams

This recipe from my friend Roberta makes a hearty winter dish that will warm you inside and out. It's just the kind of dish that my mother would have made when I was growing up, since we made our own sausages and always had some stored in the smokehouse. The smokehouse was where we'd store almost everything we needed for the winter, including sausages, hams, salt pork, and all of my mother's jars of preserves. This was before we got a freezer.

It was a funny place, that smokehouse. On the outside, it looked just like a little A-frame house. It had a doorway to go in, but no windows, so it was very dark inside. You could barely see the shelves of preserves lining the walls or the meats hanging from the ceiling. But that was all right because we knew where everything was.

Now we buy our sausages, and for this recipe you can use any type that you like. If you make it the day before you serve it, the flavors will have a chance to really mix. But it's delicious whenever you serve it.

1 cup dried white beans

$^1/_2$ cup vegetable oil

$^1/_2$ cup all-purpose flour

$^1/_2$ cup chopped onion

$^1/_4$ cup chopped green bell pepper

$^1/_4$ cup chopped celery

$^1/_2$ teaspoon salt

$^1/_2$ teaspoon dried thyme

2 bay leaves

$^1/_4$ teaspoon ground cayenne pepper

$^1/_8$ teaspoon freshly ground black pepper

$^1/_2$ pound smoked ham, diced

$^1/_2$ cup sliced smoked sausage

1 $^1/_2$ tablespoons minced garlic

Two 14 $^1/_2$-ounce cans chicken broth

3 cups sliced mushrooms (use white and/or a combination of wild mushrooms)

1. Soak the beans overnight, covered with water; drain.

2. In a heavy 6-quart Dutch oven or cast-iron pot, heat the oil over medium-high heat. Add the flour and cook, stirring continuously, until it becomes dark brown (like chocolate), for 20 to 25 minutes. (Do not rush the process and do not stop stirring or the roux will burn.)

3. Add the onion, bell pepper, celery, salt, thyme, bay leaves, cayenne pepper, and black pepper. Cook, stirring, for 5 minutes.

4. Add the ham and sausage and cook, stirring, for 3 minutes or until the ham and sausage begin to cook. Stir in the beans and garlic. Stir in the chicken broth. Bring to a boil, reduce the heat and simmer, uncovered, for 1½ hours or until the beans are tender, stirring occasionally. If the stew becomes too thick, stir in more broth (or water if you don't have the broth).

5. Add the mushrooms. Cook for 30 minutes longer.

Holiday Chitlins

Makes 4 servings

Chitlins are made during holiday time in the South and served especially on New Year's Eve. They are so popular that even in New York, transplanted Southerners call us at the restaurant a few days before the holiday looking for their chitlins.

It used to be, back in my grandmother's time, we ate chitlins right after the men would slaughter a hog. I could never watch them do it; I always had to run inside the house. After they slaughtered the hog, they would butcher it, right then and there; but first, they would slit it open and take the insides out. They gave the intestines to the women, who would clean them. Now cleaning out hog intestines is no small job. But the women did it because nothing was allowed to go to waste. This recipe is the one my grandmother would use to cook the chitlins once they were clean. You can serve this dish with rice, collards, and black-eyed peas, just like we used to for New Year's Eve. May it bring as much luck to your family as it's brought to ours.

3 pounds chitlins (chitterlings)

12 cups water, divided

1 cup distilled white vinegar

1 tablespoon salt, divided

1 ½ cups chopped onion, divided

1 ½ cups chopped celery, divided

1 ¼ cups chopped green bell pepper, divided

2 teaspoons Sylvia's Secret Seasoning or dried herb mixture (page 81)

2 teaspoons freshly ground black pepper

1 ½ teaspoons crushed red pepper flakes or more to taste

1. Carefully scrub the chitlins clean. Rinse four or five times in water. Place in a large bowl covered with 8 cups of the water, the vinegar, and 1 teaspoon of the salt. Let stand overnight in the refrigerator; drain.

2. In an 8-quart pot, bring the remaining 4 cups of water to a boil. Add 1 cup of the chopped onion, 1 cup chopped celery, ¾ cup green bell pepper, and the chitlins. Simmer, covered, for 2 hours or until just tender.

3. Remove the chitlins from the pot and chop. Return to the pot with the remaining ½ cup chopped onion, ½ cup chopped celery, ½ cup chopped green bell pepper, Sylvia's Secret Seasoning, black pepper, and crushed red pepper flakes. Simmer, uncovered, for 30 minutes longer, adding more water if necessary.

Our home in Mount Vernon, New York.

Evelyn's Pigs' Feet | *Makes 4 servings*

Evelyn Jamison

Call them mud stompers, call them hogs' trotters, pigs' feet were another thing we didn't let go to waste when we slaughtered a hog. If you've never had them, they really are tender and full of flavor. Pigs' feet are a favorite with our family, especially with my daughter Bedelia, who likes to barbecue them. In this recipe, Evelyn, who has worked at the restaurant for over thirty years and who we consider a member of our extended family, simmers them with plenty of seasonings. Serve them with collard greens and peas and rice for a real Southern treat.

6 pigs' feet, split in half lengthwise (4 $\frac{1}{2}$ to 5 pounds)
1 $\frac{1}{2}$ cups water
2 tablespoons distilled white vinegar
2 tablespoons lemon pepper
1 tablespoon salt
1 tablespoon sugar
1 tablespoon crushed red pepper flakes
1 cup chopped onion
$\frac{1}{2}$ cup chopped celery
$\frac{1}{2}$ cup chopped green bell pepper
$\frac{1}{4}$ cup ketchup

1. Rinse the pigs' feet.

2. In a 6-quart pot, combine the water, vinegar, lemon pepper, salt, sugar, and red pepper flakes. Bring to a boil over high heat. Add the pigs' feet, onion, and celery. Return to a boil, reduce heat, and simmer, covered, for 1 to 2 hours or until tender.

3. Add the green bell pepper and ketchup to the pot. Simmer for 10 minutes longer.

Evelyn Jamison and Clarence Cooper. Evelyn has worked at Sylvia's Restaurant™ for thirty-three years and Clarence is the general manager.

Me, with a barbecued hog's head.

Hog's Head Cheese | *Makes 24 servings*

Jannie "Coute" Cooper

Hog's head cheese was another thing we made after slaughtering a hog, which we did a few times every year. Head cheese, as the name tells you, is made from the hog's head and its feet, which helps it gel. After the hog was killed, we would boil up some water in a wash pot. That's what we would use to scald the pig. Once the pig was scalded, you'd scrape off its bristles. Then the men would cut the hog up and everyone would take some. Before we had our freezer, some parts of the hog were best to eat that day, like the heart and liver, which we would fry up then and there in a big iron pan. The chitlins would need to be washed and stewed within a day or so. Pork chops, ribs, roasts, and shoulder needed to be used in a few days, and the rest of the pig was made into sausages, hams, salt pork, and hog's head cheese. We ate the hog's head cheese in slices between two pieces of bread, on crackers, or just by itself. It makes a good snack.

1 fresh whole hog's head, cut into pieces

3 pigs' ears (about 1 pound)

3 to 4 pigs' feet (1 pound)

6 quarts water

3 cups chopped onion

1 ½ cups chopped celery

1 ½ cups chopped green bell pepper

1 ½ cups cider vinegar

2 bay leaves

1 ½ tablespoons crushed red pepper flakes

2 teaspoons salt

2 medium onions, cut into chunks

1. Wash and clean the hog's head, ears, and pigs' feet. Place in a 4-gallon pot and add the water (it should cover the meat). Bring to a boil over high heat, then skim the surface until clean.

2. Add the chopped onion, celery, bell pepper, vinegar, bay leaves, red pepper flakes, and salt. Simmer, uncovered, for 3 to 3½ hours or until the meat is tender. Remove the head, ears, and pigs' feet from the pot (reserving the cooking liquid) and remove the meat from the bones, discarding the bones.

continued

3. Put the meat (including the ears) and chunked onions through a meat grinder or chop finely in a food processor. Place the meat in two 9 × 5 × 3-inch loaf pans.

4. Strain the reserved cooking liquid and season with additional salt and pepper, if desired. Pour enough of the strained liquid to cover the meat by about 2 inches. Stir once, then chill until firm, for about 3 hours.

5. To serve, dip the loaf pans to loosen in hot water and invert onto a serving platter. Cut into slices.

Game

Hunting was an important part of Hemingway life, especially for the men. Learning to hunt was something that every little boy couldn't wait to grow up and do. It really gave them pride to be able to bring home dinner to their family.

My son Kenneth remembers one of his first hunting experiences, before he was old enough to shoot a real gun. I'll let him tell you the story himself: "I must have been about six or seven, and was out in the fields by our house playing with my BB gun. I saw a bird in the sky, pointed up my gun, and shot him down into the fields. But then, all of a sudden, he got up and flew away! I was so upset. When my grandma came out of the house, she asked me what was wrong. 'I shot a bird! And I know I killed him—but he's not dead!'

"'So where is he?' she asked.

Kenneth, when he bagged his "trophy buck," New Year's Day, 1990.

"'He didn't stay dead; now he's gone.'

"Now, when I kill birds, they always stay dead."

It wasn't long after that experience that Kenneth learned how to hunt using a real gun. Now, he and all the other hunters in Hemingway go out to the woods as often as they can. They hunt rabbits, squirrels, raccoons, quail, and deer. Deer hunting is the most challenging and the most frightening of all. In Hemingway, deer season runs from September 1 through January 1 and it's not uncommon for some men to put on their camouflage coats and go out to the woods every single weekend until either they bag a deer or the season ends.

Now, if you don't know that much about deer hunting, I can tell you that there are two kinds: deer driving and still hunting. Deer driving is the kind that depends on dogs to drive the deer out of the woods and toward the hunter. Still hunting is just you and your gun. Kenneth hunts with a group who drive deer. They get together a bunch of special dogs, dogs bred from other deer-hunting dogs, and head into the woods at dawn. The men walk around until the dogs pick up a deer scent. That's when the excitement begins. The dogs give a "ruff, ruff, ruff" and wag their tails and keep sniffing and sniffing until they find the deer trail. Then they really start to howl! Those dogs bark and sniff and that's when the hunters begin their anticipation, too, hearing the bark of the dogs and the crackle of the tree branches as the dogs run by. The hunter waits by a tree, heart pounding, sweat dripping from his forehead, until the dogs run the deer past him. Then he shoots and, if he's very lucky, actually hits the deer. But deer are quick and hard to catch.

I remember the first deer that Kenneth shot. He was so proud. He rode all through town with that deer tied on top of his car. I had to make him take it down several hours later. I was proud of him, too, and the venison we cooked up was delicious!

Dolly's Barbecued Venison | *Makes 6 to 8 servings*

Julia "Dolly" Hanna Flegler

Like I've said before, in the South during hunting season, there's always someone around to give you a little bit of game, maybe some quail or a pheasant or a piece of venison. You see, that's because children, mostly boys, are taught to hunt from a very young age. My son Kenneth remembers when he learned how to hunt, and I'll let him tell his story to you:

"In Hemingway, your first hunting experience is for birds, and it's a big ritual with the children. We would all go to the woods and then catch maybe one little bird, a robin or a sparrow, and there'd be maybe five or six kids. First, we cleaned the bird—the parents showed us how to gut it and wash it. Then we made sauce with ketchup, sugar, and a little vinegar mixed together. We seasoned the bird, then got the fire started. Someone would dig a hole in the ground and put in some wood chips; then covered it up with a little screen. The bird would cook on top. It takes only a few minutes for the bird to cook, first on one side, then flipped over onto the other. But that bird is so small and everyone has to share it. The littlest kids get the wings and the bigger kids get the thighs, since they have the most meat."

Luckily, now Kenneth can catch as many birds as he needs, not to mention deer and raccoons. When he does bag a deer, we always make sure to give a piece to my cousin Dolly, who barbecues it better than anyone I know. Her secret is in the marinating, which makes the meat as tender as can be. If you don't know any hunters, send away for your venison (see Note). It will be worth it.

3 pounds venison chunks for stewing	1/2 cup chopped onion
1 1/2 cups chopped onion	1/2 cup barbecue sauce
2 teaspoons seasoned salt	1 tablespoon fresh lemon juice
1 teaspoon crushed red pepper flakes	1 tablespoon sugar
1 teaspoon freshly ground black pepper	1 teaspoon seasoned salt
	1 teaspoon crushed red pepper flakes
FOR THE BARBECUE SAUCE	1 teaspoon freshly ground black pepper
1 cup distilled white vinegar	

1. Rinse the venison and pat dry. Place the venison and onion in a baking dish.

2. In a small bowl, combine the seasoned salt, red pepper flakes, and black pepper. Sprinkle over the venison and onion, covering the venison all over. Let stand in the refrigerator for at least 2 hours or overnight.

3. Preheat the oven to 350°F.

4. Place the venison in a 9 × 13-inch baking pan. Tightly cover with aluminum foil and bake for 4 to 5 hours, or until tender.

5. While the venison is baking, prepare the barbecue sauce. Stir together all the ingredients for the sauce in a 1-quart saucepan. Bring to a boil, reduce the heat, and simmer for 10 minutes. Set aside.

6. Remove the venison from the oven. Shred the meat and stir in ¾ cup of the barbecue sauce. Return to the oven and bake, covered, for 30 minutes longer. Warm the extra barbecue sauce and serve on the side.

NOTE: You can order venison by mail from D'Artagnan by calling 1-800-DARTAGN.

Mary Hanna, my cousin Julia "Dolly" Hanna Flegler's mother.

Fried Rabbit Hash | *Makes 4 to 5 servings*

Sam McCant

This delicious rabbit recipe was sent to us by my cousin Sam McCant. Like many of the men from around Hemingway, Sam was a great hunter. We would see him early in the morning, when the kids were leaving for school, on his way into the woods. Flung over his shoulder were two specially made canvas sacks for carrying back all the game he was going to catch. On good hunting days, Sam would pass by our house and leave us a rabbit or a 'coon. That's the thing about Hemingway—when one has, everyone has.

Notice in this recipe that the rabbit is simmered with salt pork before frying. The simmering both cooks the rabbit and gives it plenty of flavor. Sam says to make sure and use salt pork or unsmoked bacon, since smoked bacon would interfere with the delicate taste of the rabbit.

1 medium rabbit (about 5 pounds)
Water
1 tablespoon plus ½ teaspoon salt, divided
3 slices salt pork
½ cup all-purpose flour
1 ½ cups vegetable oil
½ cup chopped onion
¼ cup chopped green bell pepper
1 ½ cups water
½ teaspoon freshly ground black pepper

1. Cut the rabbit into 5 or 6 pieces. Place in a bowl with enough water to cover. Add 1 tablespoon of the salt. Marinate in the refrigerator overnight. Discard the water and rinse the rabbit pieces.

2. Place the rabbit and salt pork in a 6-quart pot with enough water to cover. Bring to a boil over high heat. Reduce the heat and simmer, covered, for 1 to 2 hours or until the rabbit is tender. Remove the rabbit from the pot to cool; discard the salt pork and water.

3. Dredge the rabbit in the flour. Heat the oil, over high heat, in a large skillet until the oil bubbles when some flour is thrown in. Add the rabbit and cook until lightly browned, 5 to 6 minutes per side. Remove the rabbit from the skillet. Discard all but 3 tablespoons of the oil. Add the onion and green pepper to the oil in the skillet. Cook, stirring, until the onion is transparent, for about 2 minutes. Add the 1 ½ cups water to the skillet and stir in the remaining ½ teaspoon of the salt and the black pepper. Return the rabbit to the skillet and cook, covered, for 35 to 40 minutes, turning the rabbit once or twice.

Sam McCant and Buddy Burgess at Buddy and Sarah's sixtieth wedding anniversary. Sam was Buddy's best man at his wedding.

Dolly's Delicious 'Coon | *Makes 6 servings*

Julia "Dolly" Hanna Flegler

Nobody, but nobody, beats my cousin Dolly at cooking 'coon—raccoon, that is. When I was a girl, everyone around Hemingway said that a man's not a man until he's eaten 'coon. But that was never a problem in our family, since Dolly always makes this wonderful dish every holiday, and everyone, man or woman, eats it all up.

Now if you ask where to get 'coon, the answer down South is to hunt it. You see, in Hemingway, most little boys learn how to hunt from a very young age, so, during the season, there is always someone bringing a 'coon, some birds, or a piece of venison by your house. If you've never had 'coon, I can tell you that it tastes a little bit like dry pork, although maybe stronger. It's great over rice, and even better made into sandwiches the next day.

My son Kenneth says that there's nothing he'd rather bring back to New York after spending Labor Day in South Carolina than a couple of sandwiches stuffed with Dolly's 'coon. In fact, one year, after we had all driven about twelve miles toward New York, Kenny startled us as he said, "Oh my God, I left my 'coon!" He then turned the car around and went back for those sandwiches; that's how much he loves them.

One 5-pound raccoon	**1.** Rinse the raccoon and cut into pieces. Place in a large pot with the quartered onions and fatback; add enough water to cover. Add the crushed red pepper flakes, seasoned salt, salt, pepper, and Accent. Bring to a boil over high heat. Reduce the heat and simmer, covered, for 6 hours or until the meat is so tender it is falling off the bones. Drain the cooking liquid, but reserve the fatback.
3 large onions, quartered	
¼ pound fatback, cut into chunks	
Water	
2 tablespoons crushed red pepper flakes	
1 tablespoon seasoned salt	
2 teaspoons salt	
2 teaspoons freshly ground black pepper	
2 teaspoons Accent (optional)	
2 cups chopped onion	

2. Preheat the oven to 350°F.

3. Let the raccoon sit until cool enough to handle. Remove the meat from the bones (discarding the bones). Chop the fatback into smaller pieces. Place the raccoon and fatback in a baking pan and stir in the chopped onion. Season with additional crushed red pepper flakes, seasoned salt, salt, pepper, and Accent to taste.

4. Bake for 45 minutes to 1 hour until the meat is dry (but not too dry), stirring every 15 minutes.

My brother, McKinley Preston.

Crispy Roast Duck with Apple and Raisin Sauce

Makes 2 to 4 servings

Although people in Hemingway always ate a lot of roast duck, especially during duck-hunting season, no one liked duck as much, or made it as well, as my brother, McKinley Preston.

Before he passed, every Memorial Day, we all used to gather at McKinley's house for the very first cookout of the season. McKinley loved to put on a put, as we used to say, and he served up quite a spread. There were the usual family favorites: barbecued ribs and chicken, steak, potato salad, yams, and collard greens, and then there were the special dishes that you could only find at McKinley's house. He used to hot-smoke whole salmons, roast a few ducks, and slow-bake a huge pan of beans. He also passed around a few jugs of his homemade wine, made from the sweet white grapes he grew in his grape arbor. He would make the wine the year before during the fall harvest and serve it on Memorial Day. That man knew how to have a party.

I'm very sad that McKinley died without being able to give us a recipe for this cookbook. But here's my recipe for roasted duck, which I'll dedicate to his memory.

One 4- to 5-pound duck
1 teaspoon salt
½ teaspoon freshly ground black pepper
3 tablespoons butter
3 cups peeled sliced apples
1 cup apple juice, divided
⅓ cup Cane Patch syrup or Alagra syrup (see Note)
¼ cup raisins
¼ teaspoon ground allspice
2 teaspoons cornstarch

1. Rinse the duck and pat dry; prick with a fork all over. Sprinkle with salt and pepper; let stand for at least 20 minutes or, even better, overnight in the refrigerator.

2. Preheat the oven to 375°F.

3. Place the duck in a 9 × 13½-inch baking pan. Bake for 1 hour or until the duck is tender and the skin is crisp.

continued

4. While the duck is roasting, melt the butter in a large skillet over medium-high heat. Add the apples and cook until lightly browned, about 4 minutes. Stir in ¾ cup of the apple juice, the syrup, raisins, and allspice. Bring to a boil and immediately remove from the heat and set aside.

5. Remove the duck to a serving platter. Discard as much fat as possible from the pan. Add the apples with the sauce to the pan and stir, scraping up any brown bits in the bottom of the pan. Stir the cornstarch into the remaining ¼ cup of apple juice and add to the pan with the apples. Place over high heat and bring to a boil, stirring constantly.

6. Carve the duck or cut into halves or quarters. Serve with the sauce on the side.

NOTE: If you can't find Cane Patch or Alagra syrup, try substituting Karo dark corn syrup or even pancake syrup with a little molasses added for flavor. You want the flavor of molasses, but straight molasses is much too strong.

Fish and Seafood

My mother was quite a fisherwoman in her time. She loved fishing, and she could always manage to find the time to do it, even when she was a midwife and had six of her grandchildren living with her! But fishing was her hobby as much as it was a way for her to bring home the family's breakfast.

Like all people who fish, Mama kept her bait ready so she could run off and fish whenever she had an hour. She liked to use worms, which she dug up behind the barn and stored in an old coffee can. Then she'd take her bamboo pole (we didn't have fishing rods back then) and walk over to the fishing hole. She'd put the hook, bait, and sinker on the fishing line, tie it to the pole, and cast it into the water. Whenever she caught something, she would have to throw the pole back and flip that fish out of the water. Sometimes she'd throw it so high that the fish would get caught in the trees and she'd have to cut it down.

If she wasn't catching fish, my mother was buying boxes of fish and shrimp down by Atlantic Beach when we went for the day. Shrimp was a very special treat at our house, and my mother would wait for the shrimp boats to come in so that she could buy live shrimp fresh out of the ocean. She would buy as many as she could and take them home and freeze them. Then she'd serve them for a special dinner, either fried or stewed with rice.

Catfish, which we usually bought, were also very popular in Hemingway. Most people served catfish either fried or stewed. Fish stew was a big favorite and a dish that people would make for parties. My cousin H.J. used to make a great fish stew whenever he had a party, which was pretty often, since H.J. was a fun-loving, partying kind of guy. The thing about H.J. was that you never were quite sure what the fish in your stew actually was. Usually it was catfish, but one time H.J. stewed up some shark. If he hadn't thrown such good parties, I don't know if I would have gone back after that one, that's for sure.

Bert's Catfish Stew | *Makes 4 servings*

Bertha "Bert" Pressley

Spots are most definitely my favorite kind of fish. They are what we meant when we said "fried fish" when I was growing up. We meant fried spots. My family loved spots so much that whenever we were down by the beach, my mother would buy a fifty-pound case for us to bring home. We'd clean and store them in the freezer so we'd always have a good supply.

Spots, also known as red drums, Lafayettes, and Cape May goodies, are a mild-flavored, white-fleshed fish native to East Coast American waters. Unfortunately, spots are very seasonal in New York, and so now I make my fried fish with another delicious variety: catfish. It's so tasty that it makes me even forget about spots—at least for a little while.

2 pounds catfish fillets (4 fillets)
1 teaspoon salt
1 teaspoon Sylvia's Secret Seasoning or dried herb mixture (page 81)
½ teaspoon freshly ground black pepper
2 tablespoons vegetable oil
1 cup chopped onion
1 cup chopped celery
½ cup chopped green bell pepper
One 14 ½-ounce can whole peeled tomatoes
One 8-ounce can tomato sauce
1 teaspoon sugar

1. Rinse the catfish fillets and pat dry. Season both sides with the salt, Sylvia's Secret Seasoning, and black pepper. Let stand for 20 minutes or, even better, overnight in the refrigerator.

2. Heat the oil in a large skillet over high heat. Add the fish and cook until cooked halfway through, for 1 to 2 minutes per side. Remove the fish from the skillet. Cut each fillet into 4 or 5 pieces.

3. Add the onion, celery, and bell pepper to the skillet and cook, stirring, until softened, for about 3 minutes. Stir in the whole peeled tomatoes (with the juice), breaking up the tomatoes with the back of a spoon, tomato sauce, and sugar. Cook, stirring, for about 5 minutes.

4. Return the fish to the skillet and cook until it is completely cooked through, about 7 minutes, stirring frequently.

Fried Fish | *Makes 4 servings*

When I was a girl, we'd have fried fish at least twice a week: once for supper on Friday night and once for breakfast on Sunday. For breakfast, we'd eat the fish with grits and biscuits with syrup, but on Friday we made fried fish sandwiches.

Now, there is a particular method to making fried fish sandwiches in the South. First of all, you have to use soft white bread. Next the fish has got to be hot and crisp, straight from the pot. Then you smother the sandwich with hot sauce. The unusual part for non-Southerners is that we put the whole fish, skin and bones and all, in our sandwiches.

Not that you eat the bones. No, your mouth acts like a sifter, with your tongue moving back and forth pushing the bones out of one side of your mouth as you chew on the other side. The funny part about it is that even the youngest kids can eat fried fish sandwiches without swallowing any bones. Let me tell you, God is something else.

1 teaspoon plus 1 tablespoon dried parsley flakes, divided

1 teaspoon salt

½ teaspoon garlic powder

½ teaspoon freshly ground black pepper

¼ teaspoon paprika

4 fish fillets (about 1½ pounds), such as spot fish, cod, flounder, or sole

½ cup yellow cornmeal

1 tablespoon all-purpose flour

½ cup vegetable oil

1. In a small bowl, combine 1 teaspoon of the parsley flakes, the salt, garlic powder, black pepper, and paprika. Rinse the fish fillets and pat dry. Sprinkle the seasoning mixture over each side of the fish fillets and let stand for at least 20 minutes or, even better, overnight in the refrigerator.

2. On a piece of waxed paper, combine the cornmeal, flour, and the remaining 1 tablespoon parsley flakes. Press the cornmeal mixture onto each side of the fish fillets.

3. In a large skillet, heat the oil over medium-high heat. Add the fish and cook on each side until the fish is cooked through, for 2 to 3 minutes per side, depending on the thickness of the fish. Drain on paper towels.

Crawfish Casserole | *Makes 4 servings*

Roberta Adams

Our friend Roberta is really one talented cook. While most people just use Worcestershire sauce from a bottle, one day Roberta decided that she was going to make her own. She made up the recipe by reading the ingredients on the side of the label, then guessing on the amounts and procedure.

Worcestershire sauce is one of the ingredients she used to flavor her wonderful crawfish casserole. During the cook-off, it was one of the first dishes to go, and once you see how beautiful it looks and how delicious it tastes, you'll understand why.

1 tablespoon olive oil

1/2 cup chopped onion

1/4 cup chopped red bell pepper

1/4 cup chopped green bell pepper

1/4 cup chopped yellow bell pepper

1/4 cup sliced scallion, greens and whites

1 cup Miracle Whip salad dressing

1 tablespoon Worcestershire sauce

1/4 teaspoon ground cayenne pepper

1/8 teaspoon freshly ground black pepper

1 pound cooked crawfish tails or peeled, deveined cooked shrimp (see Box below)

1/2 cup bread crumbs

1 cup grated Cheddar cheese

continued

To prepare crawfish: Let the crawfish stand in a large pan of salted water for about 8 minutes. Pour off the water and rinse out any grit. Cover and bring the water to a boil. Pour over the crawfish and let stand for 10 minutes or until red. Drain and remove the heads and fat. Remove the shells from the tails and devein.

To prepare shrimp: Remove the shells. Cut a slit down the back of the shrimp and remove the dark vein. Rinse.

1. Preheat oven to 350°F. In a large skillet, heat the oil over medium-high heat. Add the onion and cook, stirring, until the onion is transparent, for about 2 minutes. Add the bell peppers and scallion and cook, stirring, for 2 minutes longer.

2. In a large bowl, stir together the Miracle Whip, Worcestershire sauce, and cayenne and black peppers. Stir in the crawfish and cooked onion and bell pepper mixture. Stir in the bread crumbs.

3. Spoon the mixture into a 1-quart casserole. Bake for 30 minutes or until the mixture is bubbly. Sprinkle the cheese on top and bake for 5 minutes longer or until the cheese has melted. Serve immediately.

Our friend Roberta Adams.

Sweet and Sour Baked Fish

Makes 4 servings

Baked fish is a dish that my mother never made when I was growing up, since fish was usually fried and served for Sunday breakfast or Friday night supper. But this fabulous recipe is definitely meant for dinner. It gets its sweetness from the raisins and its sourness from the lemon juice, and the carrots make it very colorful. You can use several types of whole fish, including trout, red snapper, or black sea bass, as long as they weigh three pounds.

One 3-pound bluefish, black sea bass, or snapper

1 pound baby carrots

1 cup chopped onion

³/₄ cup raisins

³/₄ cup chopped green bell pepper

³/₄ cup chopped celery

2 tablespoons fresh lemon juice

1 teaspoon salt

1 teaspoon ground black pepper

2 cloves garlic, minced

2 tablespoons butter

1. Preheat the oven to 350°F.

2. Rinse and pat dry the fish. Place in a 9 × 13 × 2-inch baking pan. Sprinkle with the carrots, onion, raisins, green pepper, celery, lemon juice, salt, black pepper, and garlic. Dot with the butter. Cover tightly with foil and bake for 1 hour or until the fish and vegetables are cooked.

Kenneth's Honey Lemon Tilefish

Makes 4 servings

Kenneth Woods

Kenneth has been fishing for his meals ever since he was a child too small to remember. His grandma (my mother, Julia) also used to fish because that was how she fed the family their Sunday breakfast. In the South, everybody eats fried fish, grits, and biscuits and syrup for breakfast. So she would take Kenny down to one of those river swamps in the woods, usually to Jean's Swamp, which was about a mile from the house. It was big for a swamp, and was surrounded by trees covered with hanging moss. I'll tell you, they used to catch a lot of fish. I think Kenny was a natural fisherman, even back then. He must have been born with it. And it was a way for him to spend time alone with his grandma.

This recipe is not the kind of thing that my mother would have made for Sunday breakfast. It's Kenny's recipe, one that has become a favorite in his own family. Kenny says that the lemon tempers the sweetness of the honey, and both flavorings make this a very savory dish.

4 tilefish steaks (about 2 pounds total), or substitute monkfish
1 teaspoon salt
1 teaspoon freshly ground black pepper
¹/₂ teaspoon garlic powder
¹/₂ cup chopped onion
¹/₂ cup chopped green bell pepper
1 cup Lemonex (see Note)
¹/₂ cup (1 stick) butter
¹/₄ cup honey

1. Preheat the oven to 350°F.

2. Rinse the fish steaks and season with the salt, black pepper, and garlic powder; let stand for at least 15 minutes or longer in the refrigerator.

3. Place the fish steaks in a microwaveable baking dish. Sprinkle with the onion and green pepper.

4. In a small saucepan, cook the Lemonex, butter, and honey until the mixture comes to a boil and the butter is melted. Pour over the fish.

5. Cover with plastic wrap, leaving two corners uncovered to vent.

6. Microwave on high for 5 minutes. Rotate the dish and microwave for 5 to 6 minutes longer or until the fish is flaky when tested with a fork. If you do not have a microwave, place the fish and lemon mixture in a broiler pan and broil 4 inches from the heat. Broil for 3 to 4 minutes per side or until the fish flakes when pricked with a fork.

NOTE: If you can't find Lemonex, you can make a similar mixture by combining ¾ cup ReaLemon juice with 6 tablespoons sugar and ¼ cup water.

Kenneth's "It's Worth the Struggle" Baked Trout

Makes 4 servings

Kenneth Woods

It's a good thing that my son Kenneth, our family's number one fisherman, thinks fast on his feet. Here's a story he likes to tell about what happened to him one time he went trout fishing:

"I went up to the reservoir with two fishing poles, a bucket of sawbellies [little fish] for bait, and my rowboat. I set up the fishing poles on the two sides of the boat, and as luck would have it, both of them hooked trout at the same time. I grabbed the first pole and held it under my arm, then I grabbed the second pole and held it tight between my legs. Turns out there was a huge fish on that one, it weighed maybe seven pounds, and it was a fighter. After a good twenty-five minutes of struggling with him (during which time the other fish got away), I finally reeled him in, only to realize that I had left my net at home. Now trout have teeth and I didn't know what to do with this seven-pound one flapping on the end of the line. Then I noticed the bucket of sawbellies. I emptied the bait into the water and used the bucket to scoop up the fish. Dinner that night was worth the struggle."

---

2 medium trout (about 1 ½ pounds each), gutted and boned
1 teaspoon salt
1 teaspoon freshly ground black pepper
½ teaspoon garlic powder
1 ½ cups chopped onion
1 ½ cups chopped green bell pepper
1 cup chopped celery
½ cup barbecue sauce

1. Preheat the oven to 350°F.

2. Rinse the fish and pat dry. Season with the salt, pepper, and garlic powder. Let stand for at least 15 minutes or longer in the refrigerator.

3. In a medium bowl, combine the onion, green pepper, celery, and barbecue sauce. Fill the cavities of the trout with the vegetable mixture. Fold closed and wrap in foil.

4. Place in a 9 × 13-inch pan or one large enough to hold the fish. Bake the fish for 20 minutes. Remove the fish from the oven and heat the broiler. Unwrap and open the fish and place under the broiler for 7 minutes or until the vegetables are browned.

Like father, like son—Kenneth and his catch, DeSean and his.

Rise and Shine Salmon and Bacon with Grits

Makes 4 servings

Herbert Woods

This recipe is from my husband, Herbert. After more than fifty years of marriage, we still dote on each other just like when we kept company in South Carolina. One thing Herbert does for me every single day is make me breakfast in bed. Sometimes, in the morning when I'm sleeping, I'll feel something tickling my nose. It's Herbert, trying to wake me up by tapping me with a flower he's picked from the garden, still a little bit wet with dew, or with a piece of fruit from the breakfast tray.

Believe me, I know how lucky we are to have each other.

FOR THE GRITS
3 cups water
³/₄ cup quick-cooking grits
¹/₄ teaspoon salt

TO CONTINUE
8 slices bacon
1 cup chopped onion
¹/₄ cup chopped green bell pepper
One 15-ounce can salmon

1. To make the grits, bring the water to a boil in a 1½-quart saucepan over high heat. Slowly stir the grits into the boiling water. Reduce the heat to medium-low and simmer for 5 to 7 minutes, stirring occasionally, or until thickened. Stir in the salt and set aside.

2. In a large skillet, cook the bacon over medium-high heat until browned. Remove from the pan and crumble. Discard all but 2 tablespoons of the grease.

3. Add the onion and green pepper to the skillet and cook, stirring, until softened, for about 4 minutes. Break up the salmon and add to the skillet (including the canning liquid), and cook, stirring up the browned bits from the bottom of the skillet. Continue cooking for 5 minutes. Serve over grits.

Salmon Cakes | *Makes 4 servings*

Bertha "Bert" Pressley

This is one of Herbert's favorite breakfasts, served with hot buttered grits and mountains of freshly made biscuits. The secret to making delicious salmon cakes is to soak the bread in the salmon liquid, as my sister-in-law Bertha does in this recipe. It really adds a lot of flavor to the cakes. One bite and you'll see why they are one of the most popular items at Sylvia's Restaurant™ gospel Sunday brunch.

5 slices soft white bread (like Wonder or Sunbeam)

One 15-ounce can salmon

2 large eggs, beaten

$1/2$ cup finely chopped onion

$3/4$ teaspoon freshly ground black pepper

$1/4$ teaspoon salt

2 to 4 tablespoons vegetable oil

1. Tear the bread into small pieces and place in a medium bowl.

2. Drain the juices from the salmon over the bread and toss.

3. Add the salmon to the bowl with the bread. Add the eggs, onion, pepper, and salt. Toss to combine.

4. Heat 2 tablespoons of the oil in a 10-inch skillet over medium-high heat until the oil bubbles when some bread crumbs are dropped in. Drop the salmon mixture by heaping soupspoonsful into the hot oil (make as many as fit in the skillet without touching). Fry until browned on the bottom, for about 3 minutes. Turn and fry until the other side is browned, about 3 minutes more. Remove from the skillet and drain on paper towels. Continue with the remaining salmon mixture until it is all cooked, adding more oil if necessary.

Herbert's brother B.B. (left) *and his wife, Evelyn* (right), *in profile, about 1964. The arms gesturing on the left belong to me.*

Tuna Croquettes | *Makes 4 servings*

Evelyn Woods

My sister-in-law Evelyn Woods wanted to be sure that I included this great recipe for tuna croquettes in our book. Most people make tuna salad and salmon croquettes, but Evelyn came up with something new. She and her husband, B.B., came up with this idea out of necessity. This is their story:

"One Saturday morning," Evelyn told me, "my family was looking forward to having the usual Southern breakfast: salmon croquettes, bacon, eggs, and grits. But when we woke up, we discovered that there was no salmon left in our pantry. No one wanted to get dressed and venture into the cold to the nearest supermarket, which was many blocks away. The question was: What shall we do? We had a nice supply of tuna, so B.B. said, 'Try using the tuna in place of the salmon.' I tried it, and much to my surprise, there was not a noticeable difference other than a smoother consistency. We did not let our two young daughters know that we had substituted the tuna for the salmon, and they never knew the truth."

Two 6-ounce cans tuna, drained

2 large eggs

½ cup chopped onion

⅓ cup chopped green bell pepper

3 tablespoons all-purpose flour

1 teaspoon ginger teriyaki sauce (or 1 teaspoon soy sauce plus a pinch of ground ginger)

⅛ teaspoon ground red pepper

⅛ teaspoon salt

2 to 3 tablespoons vegetable oil

1. In a medium bowl, combine the tuna, eggs, onion, bell pepper, flour, teriyaki sauce, red pepper, and salt.

2. In a large skillet, heat 2 tablespoons of the oil over medium-high heat until the oil bubbles when a little bit of the tuna mixture is tossed in. Drop the tuna mixture by soupspoonful into the oil to make patties about 3 inches in diameter. Fry until browned on the bottom, for 1 to 2 minutes. Turn and fry until browned on the other side, for 1 to 2 minutes more. Drain on paper towels. Continue until all the patties are cooked, adding more oil to the pan if necessary.

Annette's Quick Shrimp and Rice

Makes 6 to 8 servings

Annette Dupree

This flavorsome rice dish promises that there is nowhere to put your fork without coming up with a piece of shrimp. My cousin Annette buys shrimp to keep in her freezer. That way, when her family comes to visit for the holidays, she can easily whip up this dish.

2 ¼ cups water

1 cup converted rice

1 ¼ pounds shrimp

¼ cup (½ stick) butter or margarine

1 ½ cups chopped onion

1 cup chopped green bell pepper

2 cups bean sprouts

1 ½ teaspoons salt

1 teaspoon freshly ground black pepper

1. In a 2-quart saucepan, bring the water to a boil. Add the rice and return to a boil. Reduce the heat and simmer, covered, for 25 minutes.

2. While the rice is cooking, peel and devein the shrimp (see Box, page 149).

3. In a large skillet, melt the butter over medium-high heat. Add the onion and bell pepper and cook, stirring, until the onion is transparent, for about 3 minutes. Add the shrimp and cook until no longer transparent, about 3 minutes. Add the bean sprouts and cook for 1 minute longer. Add the rice, salt, and black pepper. Cook, stirring, for 3 minutes or until the rice is heated through and the flavors have melded.

Our cousins Annette and Bob Dupree.

Seriously Spicy Shrimp Stew

Makes 4 servings

Allie Christine "Tennie" Cameron

My cousin Tennie says that she makes this fiery dish, which is like a gumbo without the okra, when the family gets together at her daughter Rachel's house in Summerville, South Carolina. The family loves to eat it with oyster crackers and boiled crabs. Be advised, though, because when Tennie says "seriously spicy," she's not joking!

3 tablespoons butter or margarine

1 cup sliced onion

1 cup sliced green bell pepper

³/₄ cup chopped celery

1 clove garlic, minced

2 tablespoons all-purpose flour

1 cup water

1 tablespoon Old Bay seasoning

1 tablespoon crushed red pepper flakes

¹/₂ teaspoon salt

¹/₂ teaspoon freshly ground black pepper

2 cups cubed, peeled potato

2 cups diced tomato

One 10-ounce package frozen mixed vegetables

1 pound shrimp, peeled and deveined (see Box, page 149)

3 to 4 cups cooked rice

1. In a 6-quart pot, melt the butter over medium-high heat. Add the onion, bell pepper, celery, and garlic and cook, stirring, until softened, for 2 to 3 minutes.

2. Stir in the flour until absorbed. Stir in the water, seafood seasoning, red pepper flakes, salt, and black pepper; bring to a boil. Add the potato, tomato, and mixed vegetables. Return to a boil. Reduce the heat and simmer for 45 minutes.

3. Add the shrimp and cook, stirring occasionally, until the shrimp are cooked, for about 5 minutes. Serve over cooked rice.

Crab and Corn Boil | *Makes 6 servings*

Felix and Sparkle Cooper

On the same weekend as the cook-off, my niece Sparkle and her husband, Felix, threw a double party at their lovely home in Hemingway. I say a double party because while Sparkle was making a bridal shower for my niece Linda Pressley inside the house, Felix was tending to a crab boil on the porch. It was a really special evening, with people going back and forth from one party to the other. And it was quite something to be in one house where bridal shower guests were dressing themselves up in toilet paper in a "wedding dress" contest while right outside people were throwing wiggly blue crabs into a huge pot of seasoned boiling water.

But that's the thing about Hemingway. People love to get together and celebrate so much that sometimes there are even two parties going on at once in the very same house! We are one town that knows how to have a good time. But, most important, we know how to share our joy with everyone around us. Stop by and you'll see for yourself.

2 gallons water	**1.** In a 16-quart pot, combine the water, onion, beer, bell peppers, Cajun spice, garlic pepper, and red pepper flakes. Cover and bring to a boil over high heat.
2 cups chopped onion	
One 12-ounce can beer (any kind)	
1/2 cup chopped green bell pepper	
1/2 cup chopped red bell pepper	
1/2 cup chopped yellow bell pepper	**2.** Add the corn and return to a boil. Cook for 15 minutes. Add the crabs and cook until the crabs turn red, 5 to 7 minutes. Drain and serve with butter and salt for the corn, and a large bowl for the crab shells.
1 tablespoon Cajun spice	
1 tablespoon garlic pepper	
2 teaspoons crushed red pepper flakes	
12 ears corn	
18 to 24 hard-shell crabs	

Antics and games, Linda's wedding shower, at Sparkle's house.

Sparkle Cooper, Herbert's niece.
She and her husband, Felix, held the Friday
night crab boil and fish fry at their home
during the weekend of the cook-off.

Crab Salad Delight | *Makes 4 to 6 servings*

Janice McGill

Although these days you can eat crab salad any time of the year, back in my girlhood it was strictly a summertime treat. That's because we used to catch our own crabs whenever we went down to Atlantic Beach, which is right near Myrtle Beach. It was about a forty-five-minute drive from our house, and when the weather was hot, we'd go at least once or twice a week to cool down in the ocean.

Catching crabs was a pretty easy thing to do. We'd make a basket out of chicken wire, then attach it to a bamboo pole. We'd dip the basket into the tide pools and just scoop up the crabs as they'd crawl by. We could usually gather enough of them for two meals. The first was boiled crabs, which we cracked with a mallet to get the meat out. The second was either crab salad or crab cakes. But in between the two meals we had to pick out the crabmeat from the shell, which took hours and hours.

Nowadays, you can just buy crabmeat already picked. It makes preparing this tasty salad, which was given to me by my cousin Janice McGill, easy as can be.

1 pound cooked crabmeat

3 hard-boiled large eggs, coarsely chopped

¼ cup minced green bell pepper

2 tablespoons minced onion

⅔ cup Miracle Whip salad dressing

2 tablespoons sweet pickle relish

2 teaspoons spicy brown mustard

1 teaspoon sugar

¼ teaspoon celery seed

½ teaspoon freshly ground black pepper

¼ teaspoon salt

1. In a medium bowl, shred the crabmeat. Add the eggs, green pepper, and onion.

2. In a small bowl, stir together the Miracle Whip, relish, mustard, sugar, celery seed, black pepper, and salt. Add to the crabmeat and toss until combined.

Side Dishes and Salads

In a way, side dishes are the heart of soul food, since no soul food meal would be complete without at least several sides for people to choose from, if not to have some of each! They add the color and spice to every meal.

Soul food is tied to the earth, and it's most obvious in the way we Southerners love to eat vegetables. Maybe it's because vegetables were free for anyone to grow. So long as a family had a little plot of land and a hoe, they could scratch some beans and greens from the soil. Everyone I knew in Hemingway had a garden, and if they didn't grow one kind of vegetable, they would trade their harvest for some of their neighbors'. So there was as much variety on our tables as there was plenty.

Planting season for the vegetable gardens began around March, when the seeds went into the fertilized ground. The first crops came up in early June, when strawberries and sweet garden peas and string beans would shoot through the ground. By July and August, most everything was ready to be picked, and we had mountains of fresh yellow corn, watermelons, tomatoes, field peas, butter beans, okra, collard greens, mustard greens, turnips, onions, and peppers! There was so much to gather and eat.

What we couldn't eat right away we would can in the early days, and later freeze, when my mother got her freezer. Canning has always been an important part of our culture. It is a way to preserve the goodness and flavors of all the specially seasoned vegetables and side dishes that are so important to soul food meals, and have them available year-round. It's what led our son Van and the family to launch our line of quality canned products nationally, since it was, in a sense, continuing a practice that the family had always done.

But, anyway, back on the farm, there are some things that weren't as good if they were canned or frozen, like sweet potatoes. Those we buried in a bank, which meant that we covered them with soil and pine straw so that they wouldn't freeze during the winter. We'd bank the potatoes in October, and keep them there until April, when it started to get warm. Then we'd move them into the smokehouse where it was cool.

Sweet potatoes are an essential ingredient in soul food, and they show up at most big meals. You can do a lot of things with a sweet potato. You can candy it, bake it and mash it, scallop it, make it into a pie or a bread or a casserole, or fry it with apples or mushrooms or raisins. You could also just toss a few sweet potatoes into the ashes of an oak-wood fire, and let them cook slowly while you sit around and tell ghost stories to one another. That's what we all did when I was a girl and the house was heated *only by the fireplace in the living room. We'd roast sweet potatoes as a nighttime treat, then eat them with milk or syrup or cracklings. They really warmed you up before you had to get into that cold bed. If, that is, my mama could even make us get into bed. Sometimes, the ghost stories scared my sister, Louise, and me so much that we would beg to be allowed to stay awake with the grown-ups. Back in the days before television and radio, people had to entertain themselves by telling stories, or lies, as my daughter Bedelia remembers it. But I guess they're one and the same!*

Van, Mama, Kenneth, and me in my mother's house in Hemingway, Easter, 1964.

Odessa Dorsey's Coleslaw | *Makes 4 servings*

Odessa Dorsey

Odessa Dorsey is our friend down in South Carolina. As soon as I knew we were putting together this book, I thought to ask Odessa for her delicious coleslaw recipe, since coleslaw is such an important part of almost any gathering. Odessa uses raisins in her coleslaw, and I think they add just the right bit of sweetness. Although we chop our coleslaw, you can shred it if it's easier.

4 cups shredded or chopped green cabbage

¹⁄₂ cup shredded carrot

¹⁄₃ cup raisins

¹⁄₂ cup mayonnaise

2 tablespoons sugar

1 teaspoon cider vinegar

¹⁄₄ teaspoon salt

1. In a large bowl, toss together the cabbage, carrot, and raisins.

2. In a small bowl, stir together the mayonnaise, sugar, vinegar, and salt. Pour over the cabbage and toss to combine. Let stand for at least 1 hour before serving.

Tina's Famous Potato Salad

Makes 6 servings

Ruthena "Tina" Stevens

Tina Stevens is our neighbor and friend down in Hemingway, and she is one terrific cook. She learned how to cook at an early age, since it was her job as the eldest daughter to prepare dinner for the family while her mother worked out in the fields on their farm.

Potato salad was one of Tina's mother's favorite dishes, both to eat and to prepare. This was her recipe, which she liked to make anytime there was a gathering of family and friends. Tina has stepped right into her mother's shoes. Now people always call her up and ask her to make potato salad for parties, picnics, and family reunions. And Tina always does.

2 pounds potatoes

1 cup chopped celery

³/₄ cup chopped green bell pepper

¹/₃ cup chopped pimiento

1 cup mayonnaise

¹/₃ cup sweet pickle relish

1 ¹/₂ teaspoons salt

1 teaspoon sugar

¹/₂ teaspoon freshly ground black pepper

2 hard-boiled large eggs, sliced

Paprika

1. Peel and quarter the potatoes and place in a 3-quart saucepan. Add enough water to cover and bring to a boil; reduce the heat and simmer, uncovered, until the potatoes are tender, for about 20 minutes. Drain and let cool.

2. Cut the potatoes into chunks or slices, according to your preference. In a large bowl, combine the potatoes, celery, green pepper, and pimiento.

3. In a medium bowl, combine the mayonnaise, relish, salt, sugar, and black pepper. Add to the potatoes and toss. Place in a serving bowl and garnish with sliced eggs and paprika.

Macaroni Salad | *Makes 8 to 10 servings*

Once all the kids grew up, except for Crizette, the youngest, they began spending summers in New York instead of in Hemingway. Since the family was all together, we could organize huge picnics for the Fourth of July, including my cousin Coute (Jannie Cooper) and our relatives in Connecticut. There would be about six or seven cars that would drive up to Roosevelt State Park or some other park, where we would spend the whole day. The adults would gather and talk and set up the food, and the children would play games and ride their bikes all around.

Of course, since it was my family, there'd always be plenty of food, including chicken, ribs, and steak, sweet potatoes, potato salad, collard greens, beans, coleslaw, and a big container of macaroni salad. I couldn't imagine a picnic without it.

2 cups dry elbow macaroni 1 cup chopped green bell pepper 1 cup chopped celery ½ cup finely chopped onion ½ cup grated carrot 1 ¼ cups mayonnaise 1 teaspoon sugar 1 teaspoon salt ½ teaspoon freshly ground black pepper	**1.** Cook the macaroni in salted boiling water for 10 minutes or until tender. Drain and rinse under cold water until cooled. (You should have about 4½ cups of cooked macaroni.) Drain and place in a large bowl. **2.** Add the green pepper, celery, onion, carrot, mayonnaise, sugar, salt, and black pepper to the bowl. Toss to combine. Let chill for at least 1 hour before serving.

Black-Eyed Pea Salad | *Makes 4 to 5 servings*

Black-eyed peas have always been a part of our history and an important ingredient in soul food. In fact, when someone asks me what soul food is, I always name black-eyed peas first, along with collard greens, fried chicken, and barbecue.

Black-eyed peas originated in Asia and made their way to the West Indies and throughout the South, where they flourished in the warm fields.

When I was growing up, we ate black-eyed peas mostly in the winter. We always bought them dried, since they didn't grow plentifully in our fields as field peas and cow peas did. But every now and then, we'd find some black-eyed peas growing up the cornstalks with the other beans (sometimes the seeds get mixed together). Then we'd eat them fresh. This recipe is meant for the dried kind of pea, although these days it's easier to buy them already cooked in cans or frozen. Get them any way you like, but definitely make this spicy salad next time you need something to serve at a picnic or for a buffet. There's nothing better.

1 ½ cups cooked or canned black-eyed peas
¾ cup chopped green bell pepper
½ cup chopped celery
½ cup chopped red onion
¼ cup chopped onion
¼ cup vegetable oil
¼ cup sugar
2 tablespoons cider vinegar
1 clove garlic, minced
½ teaspoon salt
½ teaspoon freshly ground black pepper
½ teaspoon hot sauce

1. In a large bowl, combine the black-eyed peas, green pepper, celery, and both onions.

2. In a small bowl, combine the oil, sugar, vinegar, garlic, salt, black pepper, and hot sauce. Pour the dressing over the beans. Toss. Let stand overnight for the flavors to meld.

Colorful Corn Salad | *Makes 4 servings*

This recipe is a newer one for our family, since when I was a girl, we always ate our corn on the cob. During the summer, we would go into the fields and bring back ears of corn. That was when we still had our tobacco barn. We used to cure tobacco in a barn using an oak fire, and when the oak ashes were still red hot, we'd push in whole ears of corn and cook them until the shuck got all black and burnt. That's how we knew the corn was ready, and then we'd eat it right away. We always had plenty of corn growing, since that's what the horses and the hogs ate. But we ate just as much of it as they did.

You can make this salad with fresh corn kernels sliced off the cob or with frozen corn.

¹/₃ cup vegetable oil

2 tablespoons fresh lemon juice

1 tablespoon cider vinegar

1 tablespoon sweet pickle relish

1 teaspoon dried parsley flakes

1 clove garlic, minced

¹/₂ teaspoon salt

¹/₂ teaspoon sugar

¹/₄ teaspoon freshly ground black pepper

1 ¹/₂ cups cooked corn kernels

¹/₂ cup chopped roasted red bell pepper

¹/₂ cup chopped red onion

1. In a small bowl, stir together the oil, lemon juice, vinegar, relish, parsley flakes, garlic, salt, sugar, and black pepper.

2. In a large bowl, combine the corn, red pepper, and onion. Pour the dressing over the salad and toss to combine. Let stand for at least 10 minutes for the flavors to meld.

Bedelia's Vidalia-Dressed Garden Salad

Makes 4 to 6 servings

Bedelia Woods

If you've recently been to Sylvia's Restaurant™ in Harlem, one thing you might have noticed is that in addition to our menu of satisfying soul food classics, there are also some dishes on the lighter side. I'm proud to say that this is mostly due to my daughter Bedelia. She is the health-conscious voice in the family and has really helped us expand our menus in this direction, both here in New York and at our restaurant in Atlanta. It was Bedelia who had us change the lettuce in our green salad to green leaf instead of iceberg, and she also came up with the idea for the creamy Vidalia onion salad dressing that goes on top.

6 cups bite-sized pieces of lettuce of your choice
1 cup sliced tomato
$\frac{1}{2}$ cup sliced peeled cucumber
$\frac{1}{2}$ cup sliced green bell pepper
$\frac{1}{2}$ cup coarsely shredded carrot
$\frac{1}{3}$ cup mayonnaise
1 tablespoon sugar
1 $\frac{1}{2}$ teaspoons cider vinegar
1 teaspoon water
$\frac{1}{2}$ teaspoon grated Vidalia onion
$\frac{1}{4}$ teaspoon ground turmeric
$\frac{1}{4}$ teaspoon dry mustard
$\frac{1}{4}$ teaspoon cracked pepper
$\frac{1}{8}$ teaspoon salt

1. In a large bowl, combine the lettuce, tomato, cucumber, green pepper, and carrot.

2. In a small bowl, combine the mayonnaise, sugar, cider vinegar, water, grated onion, turmeric, dry mustard, cracked pepper, and salt. Serve with the dressing on the side or pour the dressing over the salad and toss.

Sylvia's Chicken Salad | *Makes 4 to 5 servings*

When I was three years old, my mother came to New York to work as a laundrywoman. Her idea was to save as much money as she could to build a house for us when she returned to South Carolina. So, naturally, my mother carried her lunch to work. But the other girls at the laundry, they would go out to lunch, especially on payday. My mother told me that every payday, the girls would gather round her and say, "Julia, are you ever going to come out for lunch with us? It's payday!" But my mother always said no. After a while they began calling her "Cheap Julia." But my mother had the last laugh four years later when she left work and said good-bye for the last time to all the girls. "Where are you going?" they asked. "Cheap Julia is going back home to build her house," she told them. And that's exactly what she did.

My mother would always bring sandwiches for lunch, and chicken salad was one of her favorites. Here's my recipe, which I know she would have loved.

One 3- to 3 ¹/₂-pound chicken, quartered
Water
¹/₂ cup chopped celery
¹/₂ cup chopped onion
¹/₂ cup chopped green bell pepper
³/₄ cup mayonnaise
¹/₃ cup sweet pickle relish
³/₄ teaspoon salt
¹/₄ teaspoon freshly ground black pepper

1. In a 4-quart pot, cover the chicken with water. Bring to a boil. Reduce the heat to medium and cook, covered, until cooked through and the juices run clear when pricked with a fork, about 45 minutes. Remove from the pot and cool. Discard the skin and bones. Dice the chicken into ½- to 1-inch pieces. (You will have 3½ cups cooked chicken.)

2. Place the chicken in a large bowl. Add the celery, onion, and green pepper and toss to combine.

3. In a small bowl, combine the mayonnaise, relish, salt, and black pepper. Pour over the salad and toss to combine. Let stand for at least 30 minutes before serving.

Garlic and Herb Mashed Potatoes

Makes 4 servings

As soon as we added herbs and garlic to our mashed potatoes, they became an instant favorite with our customers. Some people can't seem to do without them. In fact, whenever she's in New York, Janet Jackson sends her driver up to Harlem to pick her up a plate of herbed mashed potatoes and fried catfish. That is, when she doesn't come in to get them herself!

1 ½ **pounds potatoes**

²/₃ **cup milk**

¼ **cup (¹/₂ stick) butter**

1 **tablespoon parsley flakes**

1 ½ **teaspoons salt**

1 **teaspoon Sylvia's Secret Seasoning or dried herb mixture (page 81)**

¹/₂ **teaspoon freshly ground black pepper**

¹/₄ **teaspoon garlic powder**

1. In a 2-quart saucepan, cook the potatoes in salted boiling water until tender, about 20 minutes; drain.

2. Place the potatoes in a large bowl. Add the milk, butter, parsley flakes, salt, seasoning, pepper, and garlic powder. Mash with a potato masher or fork until at the desired consistency. For very smooth potatoes, beat with an electric mixer.

Creamy Ham and Potato Scallop

Makes 4 servings

Allie Christine "Tennie" Cameron

This recipe was given to us by my dear cousin Allie Christine Cameron, whom we all call Tennie (pronounced Teenie). Everyone down in Hemingway had a nickname. Mine was Tooga and Tennie's sister Jannie is Coute or Coutsie. I don't know why we had these nicknames, but we did, and they stuck with us even to this day.

Now, although Tennie and I are cousins (her father and my mother were first cousins), we grew up at each other's sides, and we were really more like sisters, so close we were like two peas in a pod. Her children call me "Aunt Sylvia" and my kids call her "Aunt Tennie."

Tennie is a terrific cook. Since she got married young—I think she was about eighteen—and brought up four children, she's had plenty of practice. Her husband was a farmer and they had a farm about fifteen miles from my mother's place. Tennie trained to be a beautician, just like I did, and she had a shop that her husband built right outside the house in the yard on the farm. This recipe is from Tennie, and I know you all will enjoy it as much as her whole family does. Just make sure to let it stand for a few minutes after taking it out of the oven. This helps the cheese sauce set.

3 cups sliced all-purpose potatoes (¼ inch thick, about 1 pound)

1 ½ tablespoons butter or margarine

½ cup finely chopped celery

¼ cup minced onion

2 tablespoons all-purpose flour

1 cup chicken broth

1 cup (4 ounces) processed American cheese spread (Velveeta)

2 cups diced ham (⅛-inch pieces)

½ teaspoon freshly ground black pepper

¼ teaspoon salt

1. Preheat the oven to 300°F. Grease a 1½-quart casserole dish.

2. In a 1½-quart saucepan, cook the potatoes in boiling water to cover until barely tender, for 5 to 7 minutes. Drain.

3. In a 2-quart saucepan, melt the butter or margarine over medium-high heat. Add the celery and onion and cook, stirring, until the onion is transparent, for about 2 minutes. Stir in the flour until absorbed. Using a whisk, stir in the chicken broth. Bring to a boil. Stir in the cheese until melted. Stir in the ham, black pepper, and salt. Add the potatoes and stir.

4. Spoon the potato mixture into the casserole dish. Bake, uncovered, for 1 hour or until the potatoes start to brown on top.

The family at Sylvia's Restaurant™: Bedelia, Crizette, Herbert, me, Van, and Kenneth, holding a variety of our soul food favorites.

String Beans with New Potatoes

Makes 4 servings

This recipe has been a family favorite for years. Of course, we grew our own string beans. When I was a girl, it was my job, along with my sister, Louise, to pick them. We'd string them for my mother, usually late in the evening after all the chores were done. Stringing beans was a great way to pass the evening. Sometimes Herbert would lend a hand, if I was stringing them on one of the two nights a week he was allowed to keep company. We'd sit at the table with the beans piled high in the center, grab a handful at a time, snap off the stems and tips, then pull out the string down the middle. We'd keep bowls in our laps to catch the beans as they were strung. Sometimes we'd make a game of it, seeing who could string the most beans in the shortest time.

This side dish goes with just about anything, but especially chicken or fish. You can use either small red or white potatoes to make it.

4 slices bacon

¼ cup chopped onion

½ pound new white or red potatoes, cut into quarters or large chunks

1 teaspoon sugar

1 teaspoon salt

1 teaspoon freshly ground black pepper

1 cup water

1 pound string beans, ends trimmed

1. In a large skillet, cook the bacon until browned; remove from the skillet and crumble. Discard all but 2 tablespoons of the bacon fat.

2. Add the onion to the skillet and cook until softened, for about 2 minutes. Stir in the potatoes, sugar, salt, and black pepper. Add the water and bring to a boil. Reduce the heat and simmer, covered, for 10 minutes.

3. Add the string beans. Simmer, uncovered, for 15 minutes longer or to desired doneness, stirring occasionally.

Pinto Beans and Gravy | *Makes 3 to 4 servings*

Sarah Burgess

Pinto beans were a favorite workman's dinner when I was growing up. They were picked and dried and placed in large cotton sacks to be cooked during the winter. Back then, we always cooked dried beans that needed to be soaked overnight in a big pot of water. By morning the beans would have swelled up to twice their original size and the skins would be wrinkled.

This recipe for pinto beans is from my cousin Julia Burgess Wilson, who got it from her mother, my aunt Sarah Burgess. When she passed the recipe on to me, she told me about her father, who "grew up hating beans. But when my momma used to cook this dish, you could find him licking his plate because the pinto beans just melt in your mouth and are covered in a thick, dark brown gravy." Julia says to serve the beans over rice with lots of hot, buttered cornbread.

1 cup dried pinto beans
6 to 7 cups water
1 pound ham hocks or smoked neck bones
½ cup chopped onion
1 teaspoon freshly ground black pepper

1. Soak the beans, covered in water, overnight; drain.

2. In a 2-quart saucepan, bring 6 cups of the water and the ham hocks to a boil. Reduce the heat and simmer, uncovered, for 1½ hours. Add the beans, onion, and black pepper. Return to a boil. Reduce the heat and simmer, uncovered, for 1½ hours longer or until the beans are soft. If the water cooks away, add more water as necessary to the pot.

Candy Yams Soufflé

Makes 4 to 6 servings

Neomia Brown

Whenever our family gets together to celebrate, we give thanks for what we have and for one another. Herbert and I start by thanking the children for being as wonderful as they are, and tell them how much we love and appreciate them. Then everyone else has a chance to say what they're feeling and to express their love. Even the smallest great-grandchildren know that we don't start eating before saying a blessing and a prayer. Once that's said, we go on to eat. We almost always serve some kind of candied yams, since it's part of our heritage and because we all love it. My friend Neomia shared this recipe for a velvety, sweet, and delicious yam soufflé.

4 medium sweet potatoes (2 pounds)
½ cup (1 stick) butter
¾ cup sugar
½ cup firmly packed dark or light brown sugar
1 tablespoon fresh lemon juice
¼ cup milk
2 tablespoons cornstarch
1 teaspoon ground nutmeg
1 teaspoon vanilla extract
2 cups mini marshmallows

1. Preheat the oven to 350°F. Grease a 1½-quart casserole dish.

2. Peel and cut the sweet potatoes into large chunks. In a 4-quart pot of boiling water, cook the potatoes until tender, for 20 to 30 minutes. Drain.

3. Return the drained potatoes to the saucepan, but not the heat. Stir in the butter until melted and the potatoes are mashed. Stir in both sugars and the lemon juice.

4. In a small bowl, stir together the milk, cornstarch, nutmeg, and vanilla. Stir into the potatoes. Spoon into the prepared casserole dish.

5. Bake for 1 hour. Sprinkle the marshmallows over the top and let bake for 7 to 10 minutes longer or until the marshmallows are melted and brown.

Golden Fried Sweet Potatoes and Apples

Makes 8 to 10 servings

Herbert Woods

Whenever the family comes over for breakfast, depending on what time of year it is, we might serve salmon croquettes, scrambled eggs, grits, and biscuits, or smothered chicken and waffles, or fried fish and bacon. We like to serve vegetables, too, such as sautéed okra and tomatoes in the summertime, and these sweet fried yams and apples in the fall and winter. It's a recipe that Herbert came up with one morning when he was making breakfast for me. Now the whole family loves it, too.

You can also serve this as a side dish for dinner. I imagine it goes very well with poultry or game.

³/₄ cup sugar

1 tablespoon ground cinnamon

2 teaspoons vanilla extract

1 teaspoon ground allspice

¹/₂ cup vegetable oil

7 cups sliced sweet potatoes (about ¹/₄ inch thick; 3 pounds)

¹/₃ cup water

2 cups peeled and sliced red Delicious apples

¹/₄ cup (¹/₂ stick) butter

1. In a small bowl, stir together the sugar, cinnamon, vanilla, and allspice.

2. In a large skillet, heat the oil over medium-high heat. Add the potato slices, a few at a time, and cook until the potatoes are browned, for 2 to 3 minutes. Turn and cook on the other side until browned, for 2 to 3 minutes more. Be careful not to burn the potatoes.

3. Pour off any oil left in the skillet. Add the water. Place half of the sweet potatoes in the skillet. Sprinkle with half of the sugar mixture on top and add the apple slices in a layer over all. Dot with half the butter. Repeat the layering with the sweet potatoes, sugar, and butter.

4. Cover and cook over medium heat for 20 minutes.

Bedelia's Soulful Stuffed Mushrooms

Makes 6 servings

Bedelia Woods

One thing that my daughter Bedelia tries very hard to do is to create recipes that reinterpret soul food in a healthier and creative way. This recipe is a perfect example. She takes a popular party appetizer like stuffed mushrooms, but instead of using spinach or bread crumbs as most people do, she uses collard greens. The combination is unique and it tastes terrific.

1 pound large white mushrooms

6 cups water

1 tablespoon fresh lemon juice

1 tablespoon olive oil

2 tablespoons minced onion

1 clove garlic, minced

1 teaspoon Sylvia's Secret Seasoning or dried herb mixture (page 81)

1 cup cooked collard greens, drained and chopped (see page 187)

1/2 cup cornbread crumbs (see page 217)

1/4 cup freshly grated Parmesan cheese

1. Preheat the oven to 325°F and grease a 9 × 13-inch baking pan.

2. Clean the mushrooms and remove the stems. Bring the water and lemon juice to a boil in a 4-quart pot. Add the mushrooms and cook for 1 minute. Remove from the pot and immerse the mushrooms in cold water for 2 minutes. Drain well.

3. In a medium skillet, heat the oil over medium-high heat. Add the onion and garlic and cook, stirring, until softened, for 1 to 2 minutes. Stir in the Secret Seasoning. Add the collards and cook until heated through, for 1 to 2 minutes.

4. Place the collard mixture inside the wells of the mushroom caps. Sprinkle the cornbread crumbs over the collards, and sprinkle with the Parmesan cheese.

5. Place the mushroom caps in the pan and bake for 10 minutes or until the cheese and crumbs are lightly browned.

Stewed Tomatoes and Okra

Makes 4 servings

We used to eat this dish for breakfast all the time. That's because there was always plenty of okra growing in our garden, ready to cut. You can pick okra every other day, that's how fast it grows. In fact, if you don't cut the okra every few days, it will get too big and turn hard on you. Small, young okra pods, not much longer than your middle finger, are the best for cooking.

Okra is another ingredient essential to soul food.

½ pound country-style or thick sliced bacon, diced
½ cup chopped onion
1 tablespoon all-purpose flour
One 15 ½-ounce can stewed tomatoes
One 10-ounce package frozen cut okra
½ teaspoon salt
½ teaspoon freshly ground black pepper
½ teaspoon sugar

1. In a 2-quart saucepan cook the bacon until crisp. Remove the bacon from the pot and drain on paper towels. Drain all but 2 tablespoons of the bacon fat from the saucepan.

2. Add the onion to the saucepan and cook over medium-high heat until transparent, for 2 to 3 minutes. Add the flour and cook, stirring, for 1 minute. Add the tomatoes, okra, salt, black pepper, and sugar. Bring to a boil. Reduce the heat and simmer, covered, for 15 minutes.

Crizette's Garlic Fried Okra

Makes 4 to 6 servings

Crizette Phillips

My youngest daughter, Crizette, came up with this recipe during her second pregnancy, when she was craving okra all the time. Crizette has always loved okra, ever since she was a little girl. Even though Crizette—who grew up in the restaurant—never really had to do a whole lot of cooking for herself, the things she does make are wonderful, especially her okra. It has loads of fresh garlic in it (another one of Crizette's favorites), and is great to serve for breakfast with scrambled eggs, or for dinner with something else Crizette adores: fried chicken. As with all the okra recipes, try to use the smallest okra pods you can get. They're the most tender.

1 pound okra

¼ cup olive oil

1 ½ teaspoons minced garlic

½ teaspoon Goya adobo all-purpose seasoning

½ teaspoon salt

½ teaspoon freshly ground black pepper

1. Cut the ends off the okra and cut into ½-inch slices.

2. In a large skillet, heat the oil over medium-high heat. Add the okra, garlic, adobo seasoning, salt, and black pepper. Cook, stirring constantly, until tender, for about 5 minutes.

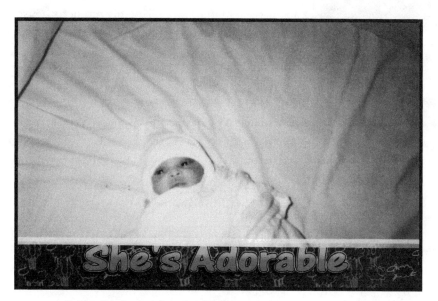

Crizette's baby daughter, Michaella, when she was a few days old.

Country-Style Cabbage | *Makes 4 servings*

Sarah Burgess

Aunt Sarah in front of Jeremiah Church.

My aunt Sarah Burgess, who is my mother's younger sister, is probably just about the sweetest person you'd ever want to meet. I can remember going over to Aunt Sarah's house all the time when I was a girl, since she lived only about twenty steps away from my mother's house.

Aunt Sarah was the baby in the family. She was ten years younger than her sister (my mother) Julia, and Julia used to take care of Sarah like she was her own child. Sometimes, when they had to walk across the fields to get to someone's house, Sarah would look up at Julia and say, "Let me get on your back." Julia always let her, and Sarah would climb on my mother's back and have a ride across the fields.

In Sarah's home, whether she lived in Hemingway or later when she and her husband, Buddy, moved to Connecticut to be with their children, there's always a pot of her delicious cabbage simmering on the stove. Sometimes she makes it with okra and sometimes she just flavors it with pork or smoked turkey. But it is always as warm and welcoming a dish as Sarah is herself.

4 slices bacon

8 cups shredded cabbage (about 1 ½ pounds)

1 cup chopped green bell pepper

½ cup stemmed and sliced okra

½ teaspoon salt

½ teaspoon freshly ground black pepper

1. Cook the bacon in a large skillet over medium-high heat until browned. Remove the bacon from the skillet and crumble. Add the cabbage and green pepper to the skillet and cook over medium-high heat, stirring, until softened, for about 10 minutes.

3. Add the okra, salt, and black pepper; cook, covered, for 20 to 30 minutes or until cooked through.

Sylvia's Collard Greens with Smoked Turkey

Makes 4 to 6 servings

We always had plenty of greens growing in our garden, and we ate them almost every day. In the fall when the collards were growing, my mother would always put some up for the rest of the year. She would blanch the leaves first and then freeze them in plastic bags. Before we had a freezer, we canned the greens in mason jars.

Greens are traditional to serve on New Year's Eve. We served them with black-eyed peas and rice. The peas stood for "p" for penny and the collard greens were green like a dollar bill. Eating the two together meant good fortune for the next year.

Although we used to cook our collards with ham hocks, these days I use smoked turkey. I think you'll find it tastes just as good as pork, and it's better for you.

3 cups water

½ pound smoked turkey wings or neck

1 ½ pounds collard greens

2 tablespoons vegetable oil

½ teaspoon salt

½ teaspoon freshly ground black pepper

½ teaspoon sugar

½ teaspoon crushed red pepper flakes

1. In a 4-quart saucepan, bring the water and smoked turkey to a boil over high heat. Reduce the heat and simmer, covered, for 1 hour.

2. While the turkey is cooking, wipe the collards with a damp towel, then wash two or three times or until all the dirt and grit has been removed. Chop the greens into ½-inch pieces; you will have 10 cups of chopped greens.

3. Add the collards, oil, salt, black pepper, sugar, and red pepper flakes to the saucepan. Return to a boil, reduce the heat and simmer, covered, for 30 minutes longer. Discard the turkey before serving, or chop the turkey meat and add it to the collards.

Frances's Old-Fashioned Collard Greens

Makes 10 to 12 servings

Frances Donnelly

We used to grow all our fresh vegetables; we had beans, peas, greens, tomatoes, cucumbers—all the vegetables we ate were from someone's garden even if it wasn't from our own. We would go down the road to our neighbors' house, and bring them some white pears or apples or whatever was ready, and they would give us some okra or some turnips. We were always sharing with one another.

One thing that we grew ourselves was collard greens. We used to pick those every day after school and cook them for supper that evening. Back when I was a girl in Hemingway, we used pork in our greens, as my sister-in-law Frances Donnelly does in her wonderful recipe. But now at the restaurant and in our canned products, I use smoked turkey. It tastes delicious, and since so many people don't eat pork these days, it means I can serve collard greens to all my customers. But in this recipe you can use either one.

6 tablespoons corn oil
1 cup sliced pork butt meat (3 ounces)
1 ½ cups water
2 to 2 ½ pounds fresh collards
4 teaspoons sugar
1 teaspoon salt or to taste

1. Heat the oil in a 4-quart pot. Add the meat and cook until partly browned on both sides, about 3 minutes. Add the water and bring to a boil. Reduce the heat and simmer for 15 minutes, covered.

2. While the pork is cooking, wipe the collards with a damp towel, then wash two or three times or until all the dirt and grit has been removed. Chop the greens.

3. Add the greens to the pot. Add the sugar and salt. Cook, covered, over medium heat for 30 to 35 minutes. Drain before serving, if desired.

Country-Style Mixed Greens and Turnips

Makes 4 to 6 servings

Jannie "Coute" Cooper

My cousin Jannie, whom everybody in the family calls Coute, may be a cousin by blood, but she and her sister Tennie are more like sisters to me. We all grew up together. I even gave Coute away at her wedding.

This is Coute's recipe for greens and turnips and it is terrific. Coute grows her greens in her garden in South Carolina. She often brings this dish when we get together, and everyone is always glad when she does. It's a nice change from collard greens.

Cousins Jannie "Coute" and Harvey Cooper.

1 pound mustard greens
1 pound turnip or collard greens
3 slices bacon
1/2 cup chopped onion
1 1/2 cups water
1/2 cup diced turnip
1 1/2 teaspoons sugar
1/2 teaspoon salt

1. Wipe the greens with a damp towel, then wash two or three times or until all the dirt and grit has been removed. Chop the greens.

2. Cook the bacon in a 6-quart pot over medium-high heat until crisp. Remove from the pot and crumble; set aside.

3. Add the onion to the pot. Cook, stirring, until transparent, about 2 minutes. Add the greens, water, turnip, sugar, salt, and crumbled bacon. Bring to a boil. Reduce the heat and simmer, covered, for 1 hour.

Coute's Eggplant Parmesan

Makes 6 servings

Jannie "Coute" Cooper

You know, if it weren't for my cousin Coute, there might not be a Sylvia's Restaurant™ today. It was Coute who got me my first job as a waitress in what was then a little luncheonette owned by a man named Andrew Johnson. Coute had been working there when she first arrived in New York. After she left she told me to go in and ask for a job. That was in 1954.

Anyway, I applied for the job and I lied; I told Mr. Johnson that I had waitressing experience. Now Johnson was from Charleston, South Carolina, and when I told him I had worked in a restaurant in Hemingway, he said, "You know there ain't no restaurant in Hemingway."

But I insisted that yes, there was a little place that sold chicken and fish. And he said, "That's all they sell, chicken and fish? Anybody can fix that."

I said, "Yes, sir, but I know how to do it."

Well, Mr. Johnson gave me the job, and several years later, in 1962, sold me his restaurant. That was the beginning of Sylvia's.

I have a lot of things to thank Coute for, that being one of them. Another is for giving us this fantastic recipe for eggplant Parmesan. The rest are just too many to name.

2 medium eggplant (about 1 pound each)

½ teaspoon salt

¼ teaspoon freshly ground black pepper

½ cup all-purpose flour

½ cup vegetable oil, divided

1 ½ cups chopped fresh tomato

½ cup canned tomato sauce

8 ounces mozzarella cheese, sliced

½ cup freshly grated Parmesan cheese

1. Peel the eggplant. Cut into ½-inch-thick slices and sprinkle with salt. Spread out on a layer of paper towels. Let stand for 20 minutes. Pat dry with clean paper towels.

2. Preheat the oven to 400°F.

3. Sprinkle the eggplant with the pepper; dredge in the flour.

4. In a large skillet, heat ¼ cup of the oil over medium-high heat until the oil bubbles when a little flour is sprinkled in. Add enough eggplant to cook in a single layer and cook until browned on the bottom, for about 3 minutes. Turn and cook on the other side until browned, for about 3 minutes longer.

Drain on paper towels. Repeat with the remaining eggplant, using additional oil as necessary.

5. In a medium bowl, combine the tomato and tomato sauce. Pour ⅓ cup of the tomato mixture into the bottom of a 9-inch-square baking pan. Top with ½ of the eggplant slices, ½ of the mozzarella, and ½ of the Parmesan cheese. Top with ½ of the remaining tomato sauce, the remaining eggplant, the remaining tomato sauce, mozzarella, and Parmesan cheese.

6. Bake, covered, for 20 minutes. Uncover and bake for 10 minutes longer.

Herbert's "Hot As You Like It" Fried Corn

Makes 4 servings

Herbert Woods

We grew corn in the fields near our house in Hemingway, just as we grew most of our other vegetables. We picked it while it was still tender, then put it up for the winter. We would either cut it off or leave it on the cob, but either way we would blanch the corn and freeze it in plastic bags. That way, we could have fresh corn (not the dried kind) when the season is out. My mother was just like the forest animals in the way she would squirrel away food for the winter.

So, even when I was a child, we could have corn all year long. This recipe for fried corn is one that my husband, Herbert, likes to make for breakfast. We like to season it with paprika and we also like to spice it up with plenty of cayenne. You can do the same, making it just as hot as you like it.

2 tablespoons vegetable oil or margarine
½ cup chopped onion
½ cup chopped red bell pepper
One 16-ounce bag frozen corn kernels
1 teaspoon salt
½ teaspoon freshly ground black pepper

In a large skillet, heat the oil over high heat. Add the onion and red pepper and cook, stirring until slightly softened, for about 2 minutes. Add the corn, salt, and black pepper. Cook, stirring, for 15 minutes.

Herbert and me in Norfolk, Virginia, 1944.

Herbert's Honey-Grilled Yellow Squash

Makes 4 servings

Herbert Woods

My husband, Herbert, is crazy about yellow squash. He loves to make it for breakfast, brushed with honey and spices and grilled until it is mostly tender but still a little bit crunchy on the inside. When he makes squash for me, though, he cooks it longer because I like it soft all the way through. You can make it either way. You can also serve it to your loved one the way Herbert serves it to me: in the bedroom, where we eat our breakfast together every single morning that we can.

Although the recipe title of this dish is "honey-grilled yellow squash," Herbert calls it "a honey breakfast for my honey." Call it whatever you want, but absolutely give it a try.

1 ½ tablespoons vegetable oil	**1.** Preheat the broiler.
3 tablespoons honey	**2.** In a baking pan, stir together the oil, honey, cinnamon-sugar, salt, and black pepper. Add the vegetables and toss to coat.
1 ½ teaspoons cinnamon-sugar (or use 1 ½ teaspoons sugar and ⅛ teaspoon cinnamon)	
½ teaspoon salt	**3.** Place the baking pan in the broiler and cook for 4 to 5 minutes. Toss the vegetables and cook for 4 to 5 minutes longer or until the vegetables are cooked through.
¼ teaspoon freshly ground black pepper	
4 cups sliced yellow squash	
1 cup sliced onion	
½ cup sliced green bell pepper	

Cassandra's Zucchini Pie

Makes 6 to 8 servings as a side dish or 4 servings as a main dish

Cassandra Woods Feimster

My husband, Herbert, is just wild about Cassandra's zucchini pie. Even though Herbert likes most everything that has zucchini in it, he especially loves the way this pie bakes up puffed and golden brown. You can serve it for breakfast or brunch, as a light lunch entree, or as a side dish or appetizer with dinner. It's at its best served warm.

4 large eggs

½ cup vegetable oil

1 cup Bisquick

½ cup freshly grated Parmesan cheese

1 teaspoon seasoned salt

½ teaspoon freshly ground black pepper

3 cups sliced zucchini

1 cup chopped onion

1. Preheat the oven to 350°F. Heavily grease a 9-inch pie dish.

2. In a large bowl, beat the eggs and oil together for 2 minutes. Add the Bisquick and beat until smooth. Beat in the Parmesan cheese, seasoned salt, and black pepper. Stir in the zucchini and onion. Pour into the prepared pie dish.

3. Bake for 35 to 40 minutes or until the top is browned and the pie is puffy.

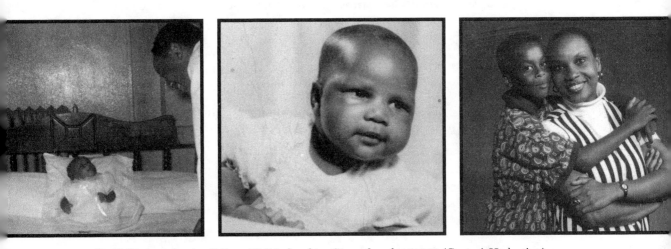

(Left) *Herbert's brother B.B. and B.B.'s daughter, Cassandra, about 1956.* (Center) *Herbert's niece Denise, when she was just five weeks old, back in 1956.* (Right) *Denise, today, and her son, Terry Leigh.*

Butter Beans and Okra | *Makes 4 servings*

Did you know that butter beans come in all different colors? In the South, we used to grow colored butter beans, which were light green with purple streaks running through them. It's best to pick butter beans when they're young, because that's when they are the most tender and the sweetest. We cooked them all kinds of ways, but my favorite is to make them with okra. You don't have to use colored butter beans for this recipe, by the way. White or green ones will work just as well.

6 to 7 cups water

1 pound smoked turkey (wings, neck, or drumstick)

1 teaspoon Sylvia's Secret Seasoning or dried herb mixture (page 81)

1 teaspoon salt

½ teaspoon freshly ground black pepper

One 10-ounce package frozen butter beans, thawed

1 cup sliced okra (½-inch pieces)

1. In a 2-quart saucepan, bring 6 cups of the water to a boil. Add the turkey, Sylvia's Secret Seasoning, salt, and black pepper. Bring to a boil, reduce the heat, and simmer for 1½ to 2 hours, uncovered, until the turkey is tender. Remove the turkey from the pot. If desired, remove the turkey from the bones and chop it and return it to the pot. Otherwise, save the turkey for another use.

2. Stir in the beans and simmer, uncovered, for 20 minutes longer.

3. Stir in the okra and simmer, uncovered, until the okra is tender, for about 15 minutes.

Lima Bean Casserole | *Makes 4 servings*

Whenever I make this lima bean casserole, I can't help but think about my brother, McKinley. He used to love lima beans, and I can remember many a time when we would sit together in the kitchen at our grandmother's house, shelling those beans and telling stories, talking and laughing.

McKinley was a real gentleman, and he looked out for me in all kinds of ways. I remember one time, after we finished shelling a bunch of lima beans, it started raining real hard. We were in the kitchen, which back in those days was built away from the house. It was raining hard and I wasn't wearing any boots, so McKinley put me on his back and carried me across the muddy yard and into the house. He was always doing things like that. He was one special person, my brother.

4 slices bacon

1/2 cup chopped onion

1/3 cup chopped green bell pepper

1/3 cup chopped celery

1 cup canned whole tomatoes

One 16-ounce can lima beans, drained

1 teaspoon sugar

1/2 teaspoon salt

1/2 teaspoon freshly ground black pepper

1/2 teaspoon hot sauce

1. Preheat the oven to 350°F.

2. In a large skillet, cook the bacon over medium-high heat until lightly browned. Remove the bacon from the skillet and crumble. Pour off all but 2 tablespoons of the bacon fat.

3. Add the onion, green pepper, and celery to the skillet. Cook, stirring, until the onion is transparent, for about 3 minutes. Add the tomatoes with the liquid and cook, stirring up the browned bits from the bottom of the pan and breaking up the tomatoes. Stir in the lima beans, sugar, salt, black pepper, and hot sauce.

4. Place the mixture into a 1-quart casserole. Sprinkle the crumbled bacon on top. Bake for 30 minutes or until heated through.

Ruth's Easy Corn Cakes | *Makes 4 servings*

Ruth Pasley

I think that no meal is really complete unless it's accompanied by a plate of steaming hot cornbread, fresh from the oven. But not everyone has time to make up cornbread and wait for it to bake before eating their supper. That's why this recipe, given to us by Ruth Pasley, who taught home economics in Hemingway, is such a joy. Since the cornmeal mixture is fried on a skillet instead of baked in the oven, you can whip it up in no time flat. And then you can still serve your family freshly made, steaming hot corn cakes with their dinner.

1 cup self-rising cornmeal mix (see Note)

1 cup all-purpose flour

1 tablespoon sugar

2 large eggs

¾ cup milk

⅔ cup vegetable oil, divided

1. In a large bowl, combine the cornmeal, flour, and sugar.

2. In a medium bowl, beat the eggs. Beat in the milk and ⅓ cup of the vegetable oil.

3. Make a well in the dry ingredients. Pour in the liquid and stir until combined but not too smooth.

4. Heat 2 to 3 tablespoons of the remaining oil in a large skillet over medium-high heat. Drop the batter by large tablespoonsful into the oil and flatten the batter into 3-inch circles. Fry until golden on each side, 1 to 2 minutes per side. Add extra oil to the skillet as necessary and continue cooking the cakes. Drain on paper towels.

NOTE: If you cannot find self-rising cornmeal, use plain cornmeal and self-rising flour instead of all-purpose flour.

Old-Fashioned Corn Dumplings

Makes 4 servings

Venice T. Singletary

When my friend Venice made these dumplings, it reminded me of my girlhood when I used to use dumplings to sop up the potlikker (see Box) from Mama's collard greens. I also used to pour a little of the gravy from smothered pork chops over them.

The trick to making really good dumplings is to cook them in the liquid of a vegetable such as greens or butter beans. They absorb the flavor and that makes them taste delicious. The directions below assume that you're making the dumplings this way.

1 ¼ cups yellow cornmeal
¼ cup all-purpose flour
1 ½ teaspoons salt
½ cup water
1 large egg, beaten

In a large bowl, combine the cornmeal, flour, and salt. Stir in the water and egg. Stir until all the cornmeal is incorporated into the dough. About 15 minutes from when the greens are cooked, drop the batter into the greens to make 16 dumplings, making sure that the dumplings are covered in plenty of water from the greens. Cook for 15 minutes.

> **Just in case you don't know, potlikker is the tasty broth that collards and other greens are cooked in. Once the greens are taken out of the pot, you can sop up the potlikker with any kind of starch. That's where the vitamins are.**

Crizette's Crispy Corn Fritters

Makes 6 to 8 servings

Crizette Phillips

Here's a dish that Crizette developed when she was expecting her first baby, Zaqura. I guess her pregnancy cravings get her over to the stove to cook up some fabulous food. But you definitely don't have to be pregnant to enjoy these golden brown corn fritters. Crizette likes them with plenty of maple syrup on top.

When I ate corn fritters as a child, we used sugarcane syrup on top. We never had to buy our syrup. My uncle Keeler had a cane mill, with a horse that used to pull it round and round to press out the juice. Then it was cooked down to a syrup and plenty of it was given to my mother. Nowadays, I either bring cane syrup back to New York with me from the South or I use maple syrup. You can also sprinkle the corn fritters with powdered sugar if you don't want them to be so sweet.

1 cup all-purpose flour

½ cup yellow cornmeal

2 tablespoons sugar

1 ½ teaspoons baking powder

½ teaspoon salt

½ cup milk

One 16-ounce can corn kernels, drained (reserve ½ cup of the canning liquid)

Vegetable oil for frying

Powdered sugar or maple syrup

1. In a large bowl, stir together the flour, cornmeal, sugar, baking powder, and salt. Stir in the milk and the reserved corn canning liquid. If you have less than ½ cup canning liquid, add water or milk to make up the difference. Stir in the corn.

2. In a 3-quart saucepan, pour enough oil to be 2 inches deep. Heat the oil until it bubbles when a small drop of batter is dropped in. Drop the batter by teaspoonsful into the hot oil. Fry the fritters until browned all over, about 1 minute per side. Drain on paper towels.

3. Serve sprinkled with powdered sugar or with syrup.

Hush Puppies | *Makes 4 to 6 servings*

Hush puppies, which are crunchy cornmeal fritters, were a treat that I'd make for the kids on Friday nights when we weren't at the fish fry in Hemingway. You see, on Fridays, we ate fried fish, and we usually ate it down at Brunson's crossroads.

Outside, there would be several huge pots boiling with oil, and that's where people would fry the fish. It was almost like a party, with everyone talking and laughing and visiting with one another.

But when we were at home, we made fish in a skillet. After the fish were fried, we'd make the hush puppies, which we just dropped right into the same oil that cooked the fish. The kids really loved them, but, then again, so did the grown-ups.

1 cup yellow cornmeal

²/₃ cup all-purpose flour

2 teaspoons sugar

2 teaspoons baking powder

1 teaspoon salt

2 large eggs

³/₄ cup milk

2 tablespoons plus ¼ cup vegetable oil, divided

³/₄ cup minced onion

½ cup finely chopped green bell pepper

1. On a piece of waxed paper, stir together the cornmeal, flour, sugar, baking powder, and salt.

2. In a large bowl, beat the eggs. Beat in the milk and 2 tablespoons of the vegetable oil. Stir in the flour mixture, then the onion and green pepper.

3. In a large skillet, heat ¼ cup vegetable oil over medium-high heat. Drop the batter by 2 rounded tablespoonsful into the skillet. Fry until browned on the bottom, for about 2 minutes. Turn and brown on the other side, for about 1 minute longer.

NOTE: These hush puppies are pan-fried, but it is also traditional to deep-fry them.

Bedelia's Sassy Rice | *Makes 6 to 8 servings*

Bedelia Woods

In the South we do not use butter on rice. We like to serve our rice smothered with gravy, topped with collard greens or cabbage, or cooked with vegetables to add color and flavor. We eat a lot of rice in the South. There's a saying that goes "Geechees love rice and alligator." Technically speaking, Geechees are the people who live on the islands around South Carolina, but some people use that name as slang for any Southerner. And that saying is pretty much true. In South Carolina, every home has rice for dinner. We may have hominy grits for breakfast, but for dinner it's got to be rice. About the alligator—I'm not so sure.

This is my daughter Bedelia's recipe for rice that's spicy and tangy and we call it sassy rice. It's slammin'.

2 ¼ cups water

1 cup converted white rice

½ teaspoon ground turmeric

1 tablespoon vegetable oil

¾ cup chopped onion

¾ cup chopped green bell pepper

½ cup shredded carrot

1 cup barbecue sauce

1 tablespoon seasoned salt

1 teaspoon garlic powder

½ teaspoon freshly ground black pepper

1. In a 2-quart saucepan, bring the water to a boil. Stir in the rice and turmeric; return to a boil. Reduce the heat and simmer, covered, until the water is absorbed, for 20 to 25 minutes.

2. In a large skillet, heat the oil over medium-high heat. Add the onion, bell pepper, and carrot and cook, stirring, until soft, for 4 to 6 minutes. Add the sauce, seasoned salt, garlic powder, and black pepper. Add the rice and cook, stirring, until all the ingredients are combined and the rice is heated through.

Vanessa's Tomato-Red Rice

Makes 4 to 6 servings

Vanessa Hill

Way back when I was a small girl, my grandmother used to grow her own rice. After picking it, she would remove the brown chaff by beating the rice until it came clean and white. To do this, she and my mother put the rice in a hollowed-out tree stump in the garden. The inside of the stump had been polished until it was smooth. Grandma and Mama would beat the rice with large wooden pestles. It was hard work and it took all day, but at the end they would get enough rice for us to use in the winter. Some of the grains of rice would naturally break during the pounding. These were called cracked rice and were cheaper than the whole grains of rice if you bought them in the store. Back then, what we called whole grain rice wasn't what you think of today, which would be brown rice. Whole grain rice was the whole, unbroken grains of rice that had been separated from the bran.

One way we all love to eat rice is to cook it with vegetables. My cousin Vanessa Hill offered us her recipe for red rice, which she makes with tomatoes. It makes a fabulous side dish to serve with just about anything. And, with its tomato-red color, it really makes a festive dish for the table.

1 tablespoon butter or margarine
1 cup chopped onion
½ cup chopped smoked sausage
One 16-ounce can crushed tomatoes
1 cup converted white rice
1 cup chicken broth
1 ½ teaspoons sugar
½ teaspoon salt
½ teaspoon freshly ground black pepper

1. In a 2-quart saucepan, melt the butter over medium-high heat. Add the onion and sausage and cook, stirring, until the onion is transparent, for about 2 minutes.

2. Stir in the tomatoes, rice, broth, sugar, salt, and black pepper. Bring to a boil. Reduce the heat and simmer, covered, until the liquid has been absorbed, for about 25 minutes.

Beefy Rice with Onions

Makes 8 servings

Modestine Woodbury

In Hemingway when I was a child, all the mothers taught their daughters how to cook at a very early age. You see, girls got married young back then, and by the time they were seventeen or eighteen, they had to know how to cook for their own family. I learned to cook most everything by the time I was twelve, but the first dish my mother ever taught me to make was rice. I was six years old when she first had me standing on a chair, stirring the rice pot over our woodstove. When she taught my kids to cook, she started them with rice, too. Rice, you see, was and still is a very important part of South Carolinian cooking.

This rice dish, given to us by my cousin Modestine Woodbury, is made with fried onions and beef bouillon. It has a lot of flavor, but it's still easy enough for a child to make. Try it served with greens, beans, or peas.

¼ cup (½ stick) butter

1 cup chopped onion

One 10 ½-ounce can beef broth

One 10 ½-ounce can beef consommé (see Note)

1 cup converted white rice

1. Preheat the oven to 350°F.

2. In a 2-quart ovenproof saucepan, melt the butter over medium-high heat. Add the onion and cook, stirring, until transparent, for about 2 minutes. Stir in the broth and consommé. Add the rice.

3. Bake, uncovered, for 1 hour and 10 minutes or until almost all of the liquid has been absorbed. Stir. Remove from the oven and let stand for 10 minutes.

NOTE: If you can't find beef consommé, just substitute another can of beef broth.

Broccoli, Macaroni, and Cheese Casserole

Makes 4 to 6 servings

Frances Donnelly

My sister-in-law Frances is a wonderful cook—so wonderful that she has even managed to find a way to get her family to eat more broccoli, which is so good for you. Her secret is that now whenever she makes her famous macaroni and cheese casserole, she stirs in some cooked broccoli before baking it. Frances says that even the youngest children in the family are happy to eat it. And the broccoli makes it so colorful.

6 cups water

1 teaspoon salt

2 cups uncooked elbow macaroni

8 ounces Cheddar cheese

4 ounces mozzarella cheese

¼ cup (½ stick) butter

1 cup milk

½ teaspoon seasoned salt

½ teaspoon garlic salt

½ teaspoon freshly ground black pepper

2 large eggs, beaten

2 cups cooked chopped broccoli
(fresh or frozen, thawed)

1. Preheat the oven to 400°F. Grease a 2-quart casserole dish. In a 6-quart pot, bring the water and salt to a boil. Add the macaroni and cook for 7 minutes, stirring occasionally. Drain.

2. Return the pasta to the pot, add the Cheddar and mozzarella cheeses and butter, and stir until the cheeses and butter melt.

3. Stir in the milk, seasoned salt, garlic salt, and black pepper. Stir in the eggs and the broccoli. Spoon into the prepared casserole dish.

4. Bake for 30 to 40 minutes or until the top is browned.

Golden Brown Macaroni and Cheese

Makes 5 to 6 servings or more as a side dish

Mattie Wilson

When I was a young married lady, we didn't use Cheddar cheese in our macaroni and cheese. We used to buy this old-fashioned, sharp, crumbly hard cheese that came in a box. We didn't buy it at the supermarket, either; we bought it at the little store at the town's crossroads. It was a real old-time general store that sold pretty much whatever you needed, from crackers and soda to barbecued pork to gasoline from the old pumps outside the door. All the kids used to love being sent to the crossroads to pick up something, since the owner, Rhoda (which we all pronounced as Rhodie), used to sell grape ice cream. It had a blue color and tasted so good. I wish I could find grape ice cream these days, but they don't have it anymore at the crossroads. They do still have the cheese. But you can make this macaroni recipe with regular Cheddar cheese, either sharp or mild to your taste.

Now, although some people at the restaurant like their macaroni and cheese to be soft and runny, the recipe for this macaroni and cheese, given to us by our dear friend Mattie, calls for it to be baked until the top is golden brown and crunchy. That's the way Mattie likes it, and I do, too. By the way, Mattie is one of the very best cooks in all of Hemingway. That's the first thing anyone says when they talk about her, that Mattie is a fabulous cook. So try her recipe. You won't be sorry.

6 cups water	2 ¹/₂ cups grated mild Cheddar grated
¹/₂ teaspoon salt	cheese, divided
2 cups uncooked elbow macaroni	2 large eggs
4 tablespoons (¹/₂ stick) butter or	¹/₂ cup milk
margarine	Paprika, for the top

1. Preheat the oven to 350°F. Grease an 8-inch-square baking pan.

2. In a 6-quart pot, bring the water and salt to a boil. Add the macaroni and cook for 7 minutes, stirring occasionally. Drain. Return the macaroni to the pot and stir in the butter or margarine until melted. Add 2 cups of the Cheddar cheese.

3. In a medium bowl, beat the eggs. Beat in the milk. Add the milk mixture to the pot with the macaroni. Stir until combined. Spoon into the prepared baking pan. Sprinkle the remaining ½ cup Cheddar cheese on top. Dust with paprika. Bake, uncovered, for 30 minutes or until the cheese has melted and the casserole is warm throughout.

Me, at the thirtieth anniversary party for the restaurant.

Biscuits and Breadstuffs

There's no one I know who could bake a biscuit as good as my mother, Julia Pressley. Whenever the whole family got together for breakfast, like during the holidays, my mother had to spend practically the whole meal at the stove, either putting in or taking out another tray of biscuits. The children always knew when breakfast was ready because they could smell those biscuits baking in the oven. The smell carried so far that even from outside the kids knew when it was time to come in. When Mama did finally take the biscuits out hot and steaming from the oven, everyone at the table would grab two or three at a time to make sure they got enough. Sometimes they grabbed those biscuits so fast that they burned their fingers. But that was part of the fun. They didn't really have to grab the biscuits like that; my mother made sure that there were always enough biscuits, enough for everyone to eat their fill at breakfast, and enough for some leftovers to eat as snacks.

There are few snacks as good as leftover biscuits. We ate them with syrup or warmed them up and put our homemade canned peaches or blueberries on top. It was a good treat instead of pie or cake, especially on Sunday.

Cornbread was another thing that my mother baked every day, and it was good with a meal and as a snack. At meals, piping hot cornbread was cut into squares and used to sop up gravy or the juices from whatever was on your plate. Then the leftover cornbread was either made into stuffing or eaten with milk. If you're not from the country, you might not know that cornbread and milk are a great favorite all across the rural South. We put the cornbread in a bowl or a cup and poured milk, sometimes still warm from the cow, over the top. Some people, myself included, like a little sugar on top. Some people eat cornbread with clabbered milk or with buttermilk. It is one of those snacks that you can forget about for months, and then when you taste it again, it tastes like the past.

There was one unwritten rule in our house when it came to cornbread and biscuits. In fact, I think the same rule applied in the homes of most Southerners. It is that you eat biscuits for breakfast and cornbread for dinner and supper. I think I mentioned it elsewhere, but I'll say it again here: In the country, we ate dinner in the afternoon. It was our main meal of the day. Supper was eaten in the evening after all the heavy chores were done, and it was a lighter meal. Now, most people, even in the country, eat lunch and dinner. Anyway, one of the reasons I think that Sylvia's Restaurant™ was and still is so popular with transplanted Southerners is that we have biscuits every morning until noon, and then we have cornbread all afternoon and evening long. It reminds people of home.

Old-Fashioned T-Cake Biscuits (Homemade Teething Biscuits)

Makes 28 biscuits, 14 servings

Annie Frazier

This old-time recipe was given to us by Annie Frazier, who is a neighbor of ours in Hemingway, and whose daughters went to school with my daughter Bedelia. My mother was the midwife in Hemingway, so it's also very likely that she birthed Annie Frazier's girls, since she delivered most of the children in town at that time. If she didn't deliver a family's children, then she at least came to their home to help if some member of the family was sick. There probably wasn't a house in Hemingway that my mother didn't go into at one time or another.

Even after she retired from midwifing, my mother would still take a day a week and go around to visit the sick. She would drive her Mercury car—she loved Mercury cars, that was a trademark of hers—up in front of a house and run in for just a few minutes to see how the sick person was doing. Then she would be off to the next house. She probably went to seven or eight houses in a day, and would always be welcomed by the family that lived there. The little children would run out of the house when they saw her car drive up and call out to their parents, "The baby doctor's coming." My mother always carried something in her bag to give them, especially if their family wasn't as fortunate as ours. Sometimes she packed cookies, or soda, white bread, or even a piece of cheese. There was always something.

Now, before you make this recipe, be advised that Annie's biscuits have an unusually hard texture, which makes them perfect for giving to babies to teethe on or for dipping into tea or coffee. They have a delicate flavor that really grows on you, and they are good to bring on a trip, or carry to someone who's sick, since they won't break apart in your bag.

¹/₂ cup (1 stick) butter	3 cups self-rising flour
1 cup sugar	¹/₄ teaspoon nutmeg
2 large eggs	
2 tablespoons milk	*continued*

1. Preheat the oven to 325°F. Grease one or more baking sheets.

2. In a mixing bowl, cream the butter. Beat in the sugar, eggs, and milk.

3. Add the flour and nutmeg and beat until combined.

4. Turn the dough onto a floured board and roll into a 9 × 12-inch rectangle about ⅛ inch thick. Cut into 28 squares. Transfer the squares to the prepared baking sheets.

5. Bake for 30 minutes or until browned on the bottom. Remove from the pan and cool on a rack.

Annie Frazier, our friend in Hemingway who makes wonderful T-cake biscuits.

Frances's Lily White Biscuits

Makes 18 biscuits, 6 to 9 servings

Frances Donnelly

Whenever Herbert and I go down to Hemingway, my sister-in-law Frances makes us welcome in all kinds of wonderful ways. On Sunday mornings, Frances calls and says, "I'm sending over biscuits." Twenty minutes later her husband, Robert, is beeping his car horn outside our door, with a covered bowl of warm biscuits by his side.

In a way, Frances is doing what my mother always did when she was alive. As we'd drive by Frances's house on our way to Hemingway for Christmas and Labor Day, we'd hit the horn to let her know we were back. Then Frances would run to call my mother and say, "Get the biscuits in the oven because they're on the way." By the time we'd get to my mother's house, hot biscuits would be waiting for us. It's the best homecoming there is.

3 cups self-rising flour, divided
3 tablespoons sugar
¾ cup lard or shortening
1 cup milk

1. Preheat the oven to 400°F. Lightly grease 1 or 2 baking sheets.

2. In a large bowl, combine 2½ cups of the flour and the sugar. Using a pastry cutter or two knives, cut the lard into the flour until crumbly. Stir in the milk, a little at a time, until all the flour is moistened but not too wet. Using your hands, work the dough into a ball, but don't overdo it. Using the remaining flour, place the ball onto a floured work surface and pat it into a circle ¾ inch thick. Cut into 2-inch circles. Transfer the circles to the prepared baking sheets.

3. Bake for 14 to 17 minutes. Remove from the pan and let cool on a rack.

Doretha's Rise and Shine Flapjacks

Makes 4 to 6 servings

Doretha Brown-McFadden

I love making stacks and stacks of hot flapjacks or pancakes. They're easy to prepare and make a wonderful breakfast or supper all year round. Our neighbor and my son Kenneth's sister-in-law, Doretha Brown-McFadden, submitted this recipe to us.

"We used this recipe when I was a little girl," Doretha remembers; "my mother made flapjacks for us for breakfast and served them with slab bacon and syrup. Slab bacon is thicker than bacon from the supermarket. You can buy slab bacon at the butcher, but we used to make our own on the farm.

As soon as Doretha removes the flapjacks from the griddle, she stacks them on top of one another, putting a small pat of butter in between each one. Then she sets them inside a warm oven (250°F) to keep them hot until all the pancakes are made and everyone comes in to eat. In Hemingway, Blackburn's syrup, which is a dark corn syrup, or Cane Patch syrup, made from sugarcane, are popularly used on flapjacks, but you can use whatever syrup you like.

1 ½ cups self-rising flour

1 tablespoon sugar

1 ½ cups water

½ to ⅔ cup vegetable oil

1. In a medium bowl, stir together the flour and sugar. Add the water and stir until smooth.

2. Heat 3 tablespoons of the oil in a large skillet over medium-high heat.

3. Add a tablespoon of the batter to the skillet or enough to form 2-inch pancakes. Cook for about 1 minute per side or until golden. Transfer to a warm plate and finish cooking the rest of the flapjacks. Add more oil to the skillet as necessary. Serve with plenty of your favorite pancake syrup.

Doretha McFadden and her husband, James.

Blueberry Muffins | *Makes 18 muffins*

Once the summer came, we used to pick our own berries back in Hemingway. We'd always have a great supply of blackberries and blueberries, since those grew wild in the woods. We would pick ripe berries until our fingers turned purple with the juice. Whatever we didn't eat right then and there we made into dumplings and muffins like these.

2 large eggs

1 cup milk

1 cup (2 sticks) melted unsalted butter or margarine

1 teaspoon vanilla extract

3 cups self-rising flour

1 ½ cups sugar

1 ½ cups blueberries

1. Preheat the oven to 350°F. Grease an 18-cup (3-inch) muffin tin.

2. In a large bowl, beat the eggs, milk, butter, and vanilla.

3. In another bowl, stir together the flour and sugar. Stir into the milk mixture until combined but still lumpy. Stir in the blueberries.

4. Spoon the batter into the prepared muffin cups. Bake for 20 to 30 minutes or until browned. Remove the muffins to cool on a rack.

Sylvia's Steamin' Cornbread

Makes 15 servings

No Southern meal is complete without a plate of steaming hot cornbread on the table. You can eat it by itself, with butter on it, or dipped into the gravy on your plate. This cornbread recipe is the one we serve at Sylvia's Restaurant™, both in Harlem and in Atlanta. Our secret is to add plenty of eggs and just a little bit of sugar to the batter, which bakes up soft, caky, and golden brown. Our customers all love it and so do we.

2 cups yellow cornmeal

2 cups all-purpose flour

1 cup sugar

2 tablespoons baking powder

1 ½ teaspoons salt

2 ½ cups milk

1 cup vegetable oil

5 large eggs

1. Preheat the oven to 350°F. Grease a 9 × 13 × 2-inch baking pan.

2. In a large bowl or on a piece of waxed paper, stir together the cornmeal, flour, sugar, baking powder, and salt; set aside.

3. In a large bowl, beat together the milk, oil, and eggs. Add the cornmeal-flour mixture and stir until just combined. Pour into the prepared pan and bake for 40 to 45 minutes or until a toothpick inserted into the center comes out clean.

4. Cool in the pan, then cut into 15 squares.

Crackling Cornbread | *Makes 9 servings*

Adding cracklings to cornbread makes it extra savory and delicious. It's something that we've done for as long as I can remember, especially just after we've slaughtered a hog.

You see, we made cracklings after the hog was butchered. It was a way of using every part, since in the South we never let anything go to waste. You'd take the fat from the pig and cut it into small cubes. These went in a big black pot and you cooked them, draining the grease every now and then, until the cubes got crunchy and golden. We'd eat some of the cracklings right there and then, and some we'd keep to use in recipes like this one.

If you don't want to make your own cracklings, you can buy them in the supermarket. They're also called fried pork rinds.

³/₄ cup yellow cornmeal

³/₄ cup all-purpose flour

¼ cup sugar

2 teaspoons baking powder

1 teaspoon salt

³/₄ cup milk

2 large eggs

¹/₃ cup butter, melted

1 ¹/₂ cups fried pork rinds, coarsely crumbled (available in the potato chips section of the supermarket)

1. Preheat the oven to 400°F. Grease an 8 × 8-inch square baking pan.

2. In a large bowl or on a piece of waxed paper, stir together the cornmeal, flour, sugar, baking powder, and salt; set aside.

3. In a large bowl, beat together the milk, eggs, and butter. Add the cornmeal-flour mixture and stir until just combined. Stir in the pork rinds. Pour into the prepared pan and bake for 25 to 30 minutes or until a toothpick inserted into the center comes out clean.

4. Cool in the pan and cut into 9 squares.

Cornbread Stuffing

Makes 4½ cups, enough to stuff a 3½- to 5-pound bird

A roasted chicken or turkey is nothing without a good cornbread stuffing. It not only adds to the flavor of the bird, it practically makes the meal. Cornbread stuffing probably came about as a way of using up leftover cornbread, since it's a pity to let it go to waste. If you don't have any leftover cornbread, you can make up a batch of either of the recipes in this book.

2 cups water

Innards of 1 chicken (neck, liver, gizzard, heart)

Salt and freshly ground black pepper

4 cups cubed Crackling Cornbread (page 218) (see Note)

½ cup chopped onion

½ cup chopped green bell pepper

½ cup chopped celery

1 teaspoon poultry seasoning

½ teaspoon freshly ground black pepper

1. In a 1-quart saucepan, combine the water, chicken innards, and salt and black pepper to taste. Bring to a boil over medium-high heat. Cook, uncovered, for 20 minutes. Remove the innards from the pan (reserving the cooking liquid) and scrape the meat from the neck, discarding the bones. Chop the gizzard, liver, and heart.

2. In a large bowl, combine the cornbread, chopped innards (including the neck meat), onion, green pepper, celery, poultry seasoning, and black pepper. Stir in the liquid from the saucepan as necessary to moisten the cornbread mixture. Use to stuff a chicken, fish, or pork chops. If not using immediately, store in the refrigerator for up to 3 days.

NOTE: If you do not want pork rinds in your stuffing, bake the cornbread without them.

Sweet Potato Pudding Bread

Makes 9 servings

This recipe is somewhere in between a bread and a pudding. It's spicy and extremely moist inside. It makes a great side dish for the holidays or for any time.

½ cup (1 stick) unsalted butter, softened

1 ¼ cups sugar

2 large eggs

2 cups mashed sweet potatoes (see Note)

¾ cup self-rising flour

⅓ cup evaporated milk

1 teaspoon vanilla extract

1 teaspoon ground cinnamon

½ teaspoon ground allspice

½ teaspoon ground nutmeg

1 cup raisins

1. Preheat the oven to 350°F. Grease an 8-inch square baking pan.

2. In a large bowl, cream the butter with the sugar. Beat in the eggs, one at a time. Beat in the sweet potatoes, flour, milk, vanilla, cinnamon, allspice, and nutmeg. Stir in the raisins.

3. Spread into the prepared pan. Bake for 50 to 60 minutes or until browned. Cool in the pan, then cut into 9 squares.

NOTE: To prepare the sweet potatoes, peel and cut 2 large ones into large chunks. Cook in boiling water over high heat until tender, for about 20 minutes. Drain and mash with a fork.

Puddings, Pies, and a Poon

If you couldn't tell from the number of dessert recipes in this book, I'll tell you that everyone in Hemingway had a sweet tooth. We ate sweets almost every day, and there were at least two kinds of desserts in our house on Sunday.

When I was growing up, and even later when my kids were young, my mother used to place the dessert on the table along with the main foods. So while we were eating our chicken or meat loaf or pork chops, we'd be eyeing the bread pudding or slices of fruit pies that were put out next to our plates. My mother never let us, and then I never let my children, eat dessert before or instead of a meal. You had to eat your regular meal so that you would get all the nutrients you needed. As Herbert says, "You didn't eat dessert to live, you lived to eat dessert."

For special occasions, like a holiday or a birthday or a graduation, there was nothing better than one of my mother's pies or cobblers. Since we canned our own fruit, we could have peach and berry cobblers and pies all year long. Apple cobblers and pies were wonderful, too, especially since my mother always made her own pie crusts. I can remember her rolling out the dough on the kitchen counter, using a Red Rock soda bottle, since they were nice and long. She didn't get a rolling pin until the fifties, I think. My mother was a champion pie crust maker. She made pie crusts from lard and flour, and was always very neat and precise in the way she rolled them out into rounds. She never got flour on the floor or on her dress. She was careful with pies the way she was careful with most things. It was part of her personality.

During the holidays, Mama would make fifteen to twenty pies over the course of a few days. There were coconut, pecan, and apple in the fall and winter, peach and blueberry in the summer, and pumpkin and sweet potato for Thanksgiving. She would find out what kinds of pies the grandchildren liked best and was sure to make enough of those so the children could take some home. She even made pies for the kids who lived in the lane! She just couldn't help but grandmother all the children she met.

Puddings were everyday kinds of desserts, especially bread pudding, which could be made from any leftover bread or biscuits you happened to have saved. Bread pudding was good served with ice cream, but then again, so are most sweets. Banana pudding was the queen of puddings, and that was a Sunday treat. Out of all the desserts, I think banana pudding was my favorite when I was a child.

My mother also made something that wasn't quite a pudding, but almost. It was called a poon, and it was made from sweet potatoes and spices, which made it very warming on cold winter nights. We ate a lot of poon in the winter, and then even more in the spring, when we tried to use up all the sweet potatoes we could before the heat came and we lost them.

My three favorite men: Kenneth, Herbert, and Van
in front of the restaurant.

Peach Cobbler | *Makes 4 servings*

We always had lots of fresh peaches in Hemingway, and a great way to use them would be to make a hot, juicy peach cobbler. Herbert likes it so much that I make it for him on his birthday some years instead of a cake. You can serve peach cobbler plain, but I think it tastes particularly delicious with a scoop of vanilla ice cream on top.

¼ cup (½ stick) unsalted butter

3 tablespoons all-purpose flour

¼ teaspoon ground nutmeg

½ cup water

4 cups peeled and sliced peaches

¾ cup plus 2 tablespoons sugar, divided

2 teaspoons vanilla extract

1 ¼ cups self-rising flour

⅓ cup shortening

⅔ cup milk

1. Preheat the oven to 400°F. Grease a 2-quart casserole dish.

2. In a 3-quart saucepan, melt the butter over medium heat. Add the all-purpose flour and nutmeg and stir until absorbed. Add the water. Stir in the peaches, ¾ cup of the sugar, and the vanilla; bring to a boil and boil for 1 minute; remove from the heat and spoon into the casserole; set aside while you prepare the crust.

3. In a large bowl, combine the self-rising flour and the remaining 2 tablespoons of sugar. Using a pastry cutter or two knives, cut the shortening into the flour until crumbly. Stir in the milk, a little at a time, until all the flour is moistened but not too wet. Using your hands, work the dough into a ball, but don't overdo it. Place the ball on a floured work surface and pat into a ¾-inch-thick circle. Cut into 2-inch circles. Place the circles on top of the peaches in the casserole.

4. Bake for 20 to 25 minutes or until the crust is browned.

Southern Bread Pudding | *Makes 6 to 8 servings*

Gloria Dulan-Wilson

As I mentioned earlier, nothing goes to waste in Hemingway. Practically everything can be made into something else. I guess we were into recycling long before it became popular. That's one of the reasons I love to make bread pudding (other than because I love to eat it); it is a great way to use up biscuits left over from breakfast, which I save in a bag until there's enough for a pudding. Since most people don't have a supply of leftover biscuits, this recipe—from our friend Gloria Dulan-Wilson in New York—uses day-old bread.

2 cups milk

12 slices white bread, quartered

2 cups sugar

½ cup (1 stick) unsalted butter, softened

4 large eggs

1 cup shredded sweetened coconut

1 cup raisins

One 7 ½-ounce can pineapple chunks, drained

1 tablespoon vanilla extract

1 teaspoon ground nutmeg

1 teaspoon ground cinnamon

1 teaspoon ground allspice

1. Preheat the oven to 350°F. Grease a 9-inch square baking dish.

2. In a bowl, add the milk to the bread and let soak for 10 minutes.

3. In a large bowl, cream together the sugar and butter. Beat in the eggs. Add the remaining ingredients and mix. Stir in the soaked bread. Turn the mixture into the baking dish.

4. Bake for 45 minutes or until browned on top and a knife inserted into the center comes out clean.

Creamy Banana Pudding | *Makes 12 servings*

Doretha Brown-McFadden

When I was growing up in Hemingway, our house was on the same lane as all my cousins' houses, so there were always lots of kids to play with. Usually, we would meet up in the yard over at my grandmother's house. During the summer, when the crops were grown high, we would play in the fields. One game that we really used to love took place in the evening when it was almost dusk. We would all go down the lane—it seemed like it was such a long way back then because we were children, but it really wasn't all that far. We all walked up toward the road, and then someone would yell out, "The boogieman's coming!"

Everybody ran for their life back down to my grandma's house. I mean, dust would be flying, all of us passing one another trying to get back. Even though we were all a little scared, it was still fun, because we knew that once we were by my grandma's house, we would all be safe. And she would have snacks ready for us. There might be biscuits and syrup left over or maybe some dessert from dinner.

Sometimes my grandmother made up a big batch of banana pudding, especially on Sundays. Banana pudding was my favorite. Even though there were ten grandkids at my grandma's house, I knew that when she made banana pudding, it was just for me. That was one thing about Grandma, she knew what your favorite food was and she always made it, just for you.

This recipe was given to us by my son Kenneth's sister-in-law and our neighbor down in Hemingway, Doretha Brown-McFadden. It tastes just like I remember my grandmother's pudding to taste: creamy and sweet with a baked meringue topping. If you don't want to include the topping, you can leave it off and serve the pudding plain. Make sure to use ripe bananas, those that have almost gone black. They have the most flavor.

1 ¼ cups plus 2 tablespoons sugar, divided	2 teaspoons vanilla extract
¼ cup cornstarch	4 cups sliced bananas (4 large or
3 cups milk	6 medium)
½ cup (1 stick) unsalted butter	2 ½ cups vanilla wafers
4 large eggs, separated	

1. Preheat the oven to 350°F. Grease a 3-quart ovenproof casserole dish.

2. In a medium bowl, stir together 1¼ cups of the sugar and the cornstarch. Place the milk in the top of a double boiler over simmering water. Stir in the sugar mixture and add the butter. Cook, stirring frequently, until the butter is melted.

3. In a medium bowl, lightly beat the egg yolks. Gradually stir 1 cup of the milk mixture into the egg yolks. Gradually stir the egg yolk mixture into the remaining milk in the double boiler. Cook, stirring very frequently, until the mixture thickens and remains in a mound for a second when dropped from a spoon, for 10 to 15 minutes. Remove from the heat and stir in the vanilla.

4. Arrange half of the banana slices in a layer in the casserole dish, top with half of the wafers, then half of the pudding; repeat layering until all the ingredients are in the casserole.

5. Bake for 20 minutes. Remove from the oven. Increase the oven temperature to 400°F.

6. In a bowl, beat the egg whites with the remaining 2 tablespoons sugar until stiff but not dry. Spread over the pudding in the casserole, return to the oven, and bake for 5 to 7 minutes or until the meringue browns. Serve warm or cool.

Mama, Aunt Janie (seated), *and Van's son, Che, about 1982.*

Mama's Sweet Potato Poon

Makes 6 servings

Gail McAllister Cribb

This recipe, given to me by Gail Cribb, the administrator of our bank in Hemingway, reminds me of my mother's recipe for a dish she called sweet potato poon. I don't know where the word *poon* comes from, but I can tell you that this dish is a cross between a baked pudding and a cake. It was one of my mother's favorite desserts to make on a cold winter Sunday, since it is so warming and sweet and full of spices that it would keep us all cozy until we had to leave the warmth of the living room and go to sleep in one of the unheated bedrooms. In fact, the only heat in the whole house came from the fireplace in the living room.

You could serve this poon plain, like we used to eat it, or with whipped cream or vanilla ice cream. It's good almost any way.

1 ½ cups firmly packed dark brown sugar

½ cup (1 stick) butter or margarine, melted

1 large egg

8 cups coarsely shredded sweet potatoes

½ cup black molasses

½ cup self-rising flour

¼ cup milk

½ cup sweetened shredded coconut

½ cup dark or golden raisins

1 tablespoon vanilla extract

2 teaspoons ground allspice

1 teaspoon ground cinnamon

1. Preheat the oven to 350°F. Grease a 2-quart casserole dish.

2. In a large bowl, cream together the brown sugar and butter. Beat in the egg. Add the remaining ingredients and mix until combined.

3. Pour the mixture into the prepared dish and bake for 1½ hours or until browned.

My cousin Allie Christine "Tennie" Cameron picking the wonderful pears from the tree in her yard.

Creamy Pear Pie | *Makes 6 to 8 servings*

Allie Christine "Tennie" Cameron

My cousin Tennie has two pear trees in her backyard in Cameron Town, South Carolina, and to this day she is always happy to share the pears she picks with all her friends and neighbors. When we were children, we regularly traded fruit and vegetables with each other. If one person nearby had a tree growing green, or white as we called them, pears, and another had a tree growing brown pears, it would be natural to swap half and half so everyone had both kinds of pears. Same with anything; we all shared what we grew and that gave us the most variety.

Since Tennie still has plenty of pears around, she's always looking for new ways to use them. She got the recipe for this pie off the radio one afternoon and has been making it ever since. It's a real favorite with her family and I know it will be with yours.

4 cups sliced, peeled pears

$1/3$ cup sugar

2 tablespoons all-purpose flour

One 8-ounce container sour cream

$1/2$ teaspoon vanilla extract

$1/2$ teaspoon lemon extract

$1/2$ teaspoon almond extract

One 9-inch unbaked pie shell (if using frozen, use a 9-inch deep-dish pie shell)

FOR THE TOPPING

$1/4$ cup all-purpose flour

2 tablespoons butter or margarine, softened

2 tablespoons light or dark brown sugar

1. Preheat the oven to 350°F.

2. In a large bowl, toss the pears with the sugar and flour. In a medium bowl, stir together the sour cream and all three extracts. Pour the sour cream over the pears and toss. Spoon into the pie shell.

3. To make the topping, in a small bowl, combine the flour, butter, and brown sugar until crumbly. Sprinkle over the pears in the pie shell.

4. Bake for 50 to 60 minutes or until the topping is slightly browned. Cool before serving.

Pear Preserves Pie | *Makes 6 to 8 servings*

Edna Bradley

This pear pie is very different from the one my cousin Tennie makes. Our friend Edna's pie is smooth all the way through, since it is filled with pear preserves instead of pear chunks. The crust isn't like most piecrusts. Self-rising flour makes it softer and more like a biscuit. The whole combination is just wonderful, and I'm very grateful Edna shared this recipe with me so that I could share it with you.

2 cups self-rising flour

¹/₂ cup (1 stick) plus 2 tablespoons unsalted butter, divided

2 tablespoons shortening

³/₄ cup milk

2 ¹/₂ cups Spicy Preserved Pears (page 233)

1. Preheat the oven to 400°F.

2. Place the flour in a large bowl. Using a pastry cutter or 2 knives, cut ½ cup of the butter and the shortening into the flour until crumbly. Stir in the milk, a little at a time, until all the flour is moistened but not too wet. Using your hands, work the dough into a ball, but don't overdo it. Take two-thirds of the dough and roll it into an 11-inch circle on a well-floured board. Fit the circle into a 9-inch pie plate. Add the preserved pears and dot with the remaining 2 tablespoons butter. Put the remaining dough ball on a floured work surface and roll into a 10-inch circle. Fit over the preserved pears and pinch the edges to seal both crusts. Cut slits in the top crust to allow the pie to vent.

3. Bake for 25 to 30 minutes or until the crust is browned. Let cool before serving.

Spicy Preserved Pears

Makes 6½ cups or 12 or more servings

Bertha "Bert" Pressley

When I was a little girl in Hemingway, my mother used to make what she called preserves. I later learned that this was also known as canning, a practical and time-honored tradition of putting food away for the future. Canning and preserving started long before we had refrigerators, which didn't come to Hemingway until after we were wired for electricity in the thirties.

Canning was a way to make sure there was plenty of food for the family during the long, hard winter, and to ensure that what we gathered from the harvest did not go to waste. Practically every type of fruit and vegetable can be preserved, and we put up pears, apples, grapes, peaches, plums, butter beans, lima beans, collard greens, tomatoes, okra, turnips, corn, carrots, and whatever else we grew on the farm.

These preserved pears are spicy and delicious, especially when served cold (which back then meant all winter long, since the preserves were stored in an unheated smokehouse). You don't need anything else but a spoon to enjoy this wonderful treat.

---

10 firm (but not hard) pears, peeled

4 cups sugar

5 whole cinnamon sticks

1. Core and quarter the pears. Place in a large bowl. Sprinkle with the sugar, tossing the pears gently. Let stand overnight.

2. Transfer the pears, sugar, and cinnamon sticks to a 5- to 6-quart pot. Bring to a boil. Reduce the heat and simmer for 1 to 1½ hours or until the pears are tender and totally translucent, stirring occasionally with a wooden spoon.

3. Cool and place in preserving jars, following jar directions for safe preserving.

Sweet and Lovely Pecan Pie

Makes 6 to 8 servings

Ruby Love Dulan

When my mother built our house back in 1933, she planted our pecan trees. I had always wanted to grow pecan trees because I love pecans, and then I only got them once a year at Christmastime. I remember when my mother put those trees in. She said to me, "Sylvia, now you won't have to worry about getting pecans," and I said, "But when will the pecans start to come?" That's when she told me that the trees would take eight years to bear. And I thought I would die because I didn't see how in the world I could wait that long.

Of course, once the trees did start to bear, we had plenty of pecans, which we made into pies, cakes, and cookies, or we just ate them from the shells while sitting under those pecan trees. There's nothing so sweet as a handful of just-shelled pecans from your very own trees.

But if you don't have pecan trees in your yard, you can buy them and make this sweet pie. It's a recipe from Ruby Love Dulan, who's the mother of one of our friends.

½ cup sugar

2 tablespoons cornstarch

½ cup water

3 large eggs

1 teaspoon vanilla extract

1 cup dark corn syrup

¼ cup (½ stick) unsalted butter or margarine

1½ to 2 cups pecan halves

One 9-inch unbaked pie shell (if using frozen, use a 9-inch deep-dish pie shell)

1. Preheat the oven to 350°F.

2. In a medium bowl, mix the sugar and cornstarch thoroughly. Stir in the water; set aside.

3. In a medium bowl, using a whisk, beat the eggs and vanilla together. Gradually stir in the corn syrup.

4. In a 2-quart saucepan, melt the butter over medium heat. Stir in the water-sugar-cornstarch mixture, then the egg mixture. Continue cooking until the mixture has a puddinglike consistency, just before it boils, for about 7 minutes. Remove from the heat.

5. Arrange a layer of pecans on the pastry in the bottom of the pie dish, pressing the nuts into the dough. Pour the filling over the nuts, then arrange as many of the remaining pecans as necessary on top of the filling.

6. Bake for 35 to 45 minutes or until a knife inserted into the center comes out clean. Cool.

Me, Herbert, and Van, standing in the fields near the house in Hemingway. Those are the pecan trees that my mother planted when she built her house in 1933.

Sweet Potato Pie | *Makes 8 servings*

Frances Donnelly

If you're not sure what the difference between a sweet potato and yam is, you are not alone. That's because most people use the terms interchangeably, and what the supermarket stocks as canned yams are almost always sweet potatoes. Botanically, though, they are different vegetables.

Sweet potatoes have probably been so popular in the South, since they reminded the slaves of the yams they used to eat in Africa. So the first African Americans adapted sweet potatoes to their traditional yam recipes. This may account for some of the mix-up.

Well, whatever you call them (and we all know what we mean), sweet potato pie is one of my favorite ways to eat them, especially my sister-in-law Frances's version.

2 quarts water

1 pound sweet potatoes, peeled

1/2 cup (1 stick) unsalted butter

3/4 cup sugar

1/2 teaspoon ground nutmeg

1/4 teaspoon vanilla extract

1/3 cup evaporated milk

2 large eggs, beaten

One 9-inch unbaked pie shell (if using frozen, use a 9-inch deep-dish pie shell)

1. Preheat the oven to 375°F.

2. In a 3-quart saucepan over high heat, bring the water to a boil.

3. Cut the potatoes into large chunks. Add the potatoes to the boiling water and cook, uncovered, until tender when pierced with a fork, for 20 to 30 minutes; drain well. Return the potatoes to the empty pot (but not the heat) and stir in the butter until melted. Stir in the sugar, nutmeg, and vanilla. Stir in the milk until the mixture is pretty smooth. Cool.

4. Add the beaten eggs and pour the mixture into the piecrust. Bake for 35 to 45 minutes or until browned. Cool before serving.

Vanessa's Apple Pie | *Makes 6 to 8 servings*

Vanessa Hill

My mother and I made a lot of apple pies down in Hemingway; in the fall, there were plenty of apples from our trees to use up. It was a favorite dessert to serve on Sundays after dinner. You see, on Sundays, after a big dinner in the middle of the day, we never really ate much more than a snack for supper. And there is no better snack than left-over apple pie.

This recipe is a little different from the apple pies my mother and I made. It's from my cousin Vanessa, who has grown up to be quite a cook. She uses a little bit of pineapple juice and vanilla with the apples, and I love the way it brings out their flavor.

1 1/2 cups sugar

3 tablespoons unsalted butter, softened

1 large egg

3 tablespoons all-purpose flour

2 tablespoons pineapple juice

1/2 teaspoon ground cinnamon

1/2 teaspoon ground ginger

1/2 teaspoon ground nutmeg

1/2 teaspoon vanilla extract

5 cups sliced, peeled apples (1 1/2 pounds)

Two unbaked 9-inch pie shells (if using frozen, use 9-inch deep-dish pie shells)

1. Preheat the oven to 350°F.

2. In a medium bowl, beat the sugar with the butter until combined. Beat in the egg. Beat in the flour, pineapple juice, cinnamon, ginger, nutmeg, and vanilla.

3. Place the apple slices in one of the piecrusts. Spoon the sugar-spice mixture over the apples. Cover with the second crust and crimp the edges to seal. Prick with a fork to vent.

4. Bake for 50 minutes to 1 hour or until the crust is golden. Cool.

Southern-Style Coconut Custard Pie

Makes 6 to 8 servings

Frances Donnelly

In our family, Labor Day was almost as big a holiday as Christmas. That's because when Herbert and I were living in New York, working all hours and trying to grow the restaurant, we sent the children to South Carolina to stay with my mother during the summers.

Labor Day was when we drove down to Hemingway to pick up the kids. There was always a big celebration, with parties lasting the whole weekend. In order to feed everyone, my mother began her baking the week before. She made dozens of pies and cakes, enough so that when we left for New York, each of the children would get to take home a dessert. My mother would pack up the whole cake or pie, and there would never be any arguing, since each child got their favorite.

I don't remember which one of the children took home a coconut pie, but I do know that it was a definite family favorite. This is my sister-in-law Frances's recipe and it is every bit as sweet and delicious as I remember my mother's pie to have been.

1 ⅓ cups sugar

½ cup (1 stick) unsalted butter

3 large eggs

One 14-ounce bag sweetened flaked coconut

1 ½ cups milk

¼ cup evaporated milk

1 ½ teaspoons vanilla extract

1 ½ tablespoons all-purpose flour

Two unbaked 9-inch pie shells (if using frozen, use 9-inch deep-dish pie shells)

1. Preheat the oven to 350°F.

2. In a large bowl, cream the sugar and butter together for 5 minutes. Beat in the eggs one at a time. Beat in the coconut alternately with the milk and evaporated milk. Beat in the vanilla. Beat in the flour.

3. Pour into the prepared piecrusts. Bake for 20 minutes. Increase the heat to 400°F and bake for 20 minutes longer. Cool before serving.

Sweet Cakes, Sugar Cookies, and Lemonade

When the holiday season approached, my mother started making her cakes, especially the fruit and nut cakes, which had to be set aside to age before you could eat them. My mother was very particular about the way she made her cakes. She had an old electric mixer which I had given her in the 1950s, and she used that mixer for over thirty years until she died. In fact, we still have that mixer in the kitchen of her old house and it works just fine. My mother really knew how to take care of her things.

My mother would mix up all different kinds of cake batters in her heavy glass mixing bowl. She loved to make layer cakes and coconut cakes, spice cakes and chocolate cakes, and rich fruitcakes with rum in them for Christmas.

But of all the cakes, pound cakes were and probably still are the most popular. No matter what season it is or what holiday, there are always several different kinds of pound cakes served at get-togethers. Pound cakes are popular for many different reasons. They are very versatile—you can add nuts or raisins or spices to the batter and make different kinds of cakes using the same basic recipe. You can slice and fill pound cakes—because they are usually so plain and simple they go with any kind of jelly or frosting. You can make pound cakes in advance, and they get even better if you let them sit overnight before you cut them. And pound cakes, all by themselves, are great to carry with you, since they won't fall apart. You can take them on a train or a plane, or bring them to a picnic or a party without worry.

Leftover pound cake was one of our favorite nighttime snacks in Hemingway. It never needed anything more than a glass of milk to go with it, although my mother liked to keep some ice cream in the house to serve with leftover cakes at night. We also ate leftover cakes in the afternoon with a cup of coffee, as a way to revive our energy for the rest of the day.

And last but not least . . .

If you were wondering why lemonade is in this chapter, I can tell you that part of the reason is that we couldn't think of anywhere else to put it. But there's another reason, too: No matter what you serve and no matter when, nothing complements soul food as well as a tall, cold glass of lemonade.

It used to be that lemonade was a special-occasion treat that you got during a church picnic or on a holiday. That's because before everyone had a freezer, ice had to be carried from the icehouse in town. In the summer, you needed pounds and pounds of it, since the sun made it melt so quickly. And you certainly couldn't have lemonade *without ice. So whoever made the lemonade for the picnic had another job, too, and that was to go and get the ice. That may be why the lemonade maker was always a man, even though the women did most of the cooking for the picnics.*

Each church had its own lemonade maker. We had Thomas Cooper, and down in Friendship, where I had many relatives, my uncle Keeler and his cousin Blake made the lemonade when I was growing up. After Keeler died, and his wife, my aunt Annie, had trouble getting around in her later years (she lived to be one hundred), the new lemonade maker, Murray Nesmith, would always save a pitcher of lemonade and ice and bring it to her home. Luckily, she lived right next to the church.

*Longevity runs in the family. Here's my aunt Annie at her
one hundredth birthday party. But she wasn't the only one to live to 100;
my uncle Harry McKnight lived to 101 and my great-grandfather
Prince McKnight lived to 104.*

Vernell Bishop's Luscious Cheesecake

Makes 8 to 12 servings

Vernell Bishop

My cousin and longtime employee Vernell gave us a recipe for an interesting kind of cheesecake. It's smooth and creamy without being dense, almost like a rich cheese custard. Just as soon as I tasted it I knew that it would soon become a Woods family favorite. And I was right.

1 ⅓ cups graham cracker crumbs

2 tablespoons sugar plus

¾ cup sugar, divided

⅓ cup melted butter

Two 8-ounce packages
cream cheese, softened

2 large eggs

One 16-ounce container sour cream

½ cup heavy cream

2 tablespoons all-purpose flour

2 teaspoons lemon juice

1 teaspoon vanilla extract

1. Preheat the oven to 350°F. Grease a 9-inch springform pan.

2. In a large bowl, stir together the graham cracker crumbs and 2 tablespoons of the sugar. Add the butter and stir until combined. Press the mixture into the springform pan.

3. In a large bowl, beat the cream cheese with the remaining ¾ cup sugar until light and fluffy. Beat in the eggs, then the sour cream, heavy cream, flour, lemon juice, and vanilla. Pour onto the graham cracker crust.

4. Bake for 1 hour and 10 minutes. Turn off the heat and leave in the oven for 1 hour longer. Remove to the refrigerator and chill.

Banana Pound Cake | *Makes 12 to 16 servings*

For years, my mother made her own butter at home. She made most of it right before Christmas, since that's the time of year when she baked almost every day.

Churning butter was a big job, and everyone staying at my mother's house would help. She would set us up at night after supper. You'd put a towel on your lap and she'd put cream in a jar and you'd shake it up and down against your leg. "Come, butter, come; come, butter, come," that's what you'd say as you shook. Everyone would have a jar and you'd shake that cream until the butter came. Even the little ones had their own jars of cream, but after a while my mother took the jars away from them, gave each jar a few great shakes, and the cream would immediately turn to butter. She really had a knack for it.

Once the butter was made, Christmas baking began. She made dozens and dozens of cakes and pies. This cake was one of my favorites. It's quick to make and has a terrific flavor, but you have to use really ripe bananas. Buy them a few days before you want to make the cake, then let them sit until they are covered with black specks. That's when they taste the best.

2 cups (4 sticks) unsalted butter

2 cups sugar

4 large eggs

4 cups self-rising flour, divided

2 cups mashed ripe bananas (6 to 7 medium bananas)

1. Preheat the oven to 350°F. Heavily grease and flour a 10-inch Bundt pan.

2. In a large bowl, cream together the butter and sugar. Beat in the eggs. Beat in 2 cups of the flour, then beat in the bananas. Beat in the remaining 2 cups of flour.

3. Pour the batter into the prepared pan and bake for 1 hour or until a wooden pick inserted into the middle comes out clean. Turn onto a rack to cool.

Sour Cream Pound Cake | *Makes 16 servings*

Annette Dupree

When I was a child, we did our work according to the seasons. In the spring and summer, we worked in the fields; in the late summer, we began the canning; and in the fall, beginning from when the children went back to school in September, we made quilts to keep us warm all winter long.

Quilting was a favorite chore to do, since all the women got together and made a party out of the work. During the year, we would save all the reusable cloth from old clothes and blankets, or sometimes we'd get remnants from a fabric company. Even the children could help, since they could imagine wonderful designs and patterns to use out of all the different colored pieces that the women collected. After the pattern was figured out, we would piece the quilt at home on rainy days when we couldn't work in the fields. Then everyone would get together to finish them. On a good day, we'd be able to do two quilts. No one ever had to buy quilts in Hemingway, since it was such a pleasure to make them. We'd all catch up with one another and laugh and tell stories to the children.

After the work was done, supper began. There were all kinds of delicious dishes, and all the women would bring something special for everyone to share. Pound cakes were a favorite quilting party dessert, since they were easy to carry. My cousin Annette's pound cake, moist and just a little bit tangy from the sour cream, would have certainly been a hit. It is—wherever she serves it now; that's for sure.

2 cups all-purpose flour	3 cups sugar
1 cup self-rising flour	6 large eggs
One 3.4-ounce package	One 5-ounce can evaporated milk
vanilla instant pudding	One 8-ounce container sour cream
2 cups (4 sticks) unsalted butter, softened	1 tablespoon vanilla extract

1. Preheat the oven to 325°F. Heavily grease and flour a 10-inch tube pan.

2. In a medium bowl or on a piece of waxed paper, sift together the all-purpose flour, self-rising flour, and pudding mix.

3. In a large bowl, beat the butter with an electric mixer for 3 minutes. Add the sugar and beat for 5 minutes. Add the eggs, one at a time, then the evaporated milk. Add the flour mixture and beat until smooth. Add the sour cream and vanilla and beat until combined.

4. Bake for 1 hour and 45 minutes or until a wooden pick inserted into the center of the cake comes out clean. Turn onto a rack to cool.

Raisin Pound Cake | *Makes 16 to 20 servings*

Shirley "Jean" Pressley Nesmith

We have a new tradition in our family, and that is caroling on Christmas Eve. It wasn't something I did when I was young; it all started soon after my mother's death. My son Kenneth, in particular, was saddened by his grandmother's passing, and so he decided to go over to her old house and put up some lights. It just seemed so lonely. Somehow while he was over there, he and his wife, Sylvia, just started singing Christmas carols to bring some warmth into those seemingly cold rooms.

We've sung carols at her house every Christmas Eve since, and now we light candles and invite Sylvia's family, the Browns, over to sing in honor of my mother, Julia, and all the other people in our lives who have passed on. When Mama was alive, we'd spend Christmas Eve eating some of the food that she had prepared for us during the weeks before our arrival from New York. But now we keep things simple, and just have some punch, snacks, and cake to give us energy for all that singing. Our cousin Jean's raisin pound cake is just the kind of treat that my mother would have liked to serve during the holidays, since it's dense and sweet and filled with raisins.

If you do make it, be sure to think of Julia Pressley.

3 cups plus 2 tablespoons sifted all-purpose flour, divided	One 3-ounce package cream cheese softened
1/2 teaspoon salt	3 cups sugar
1 1/2 cups raisins	6 large eggs
1 1/2 cups (3 sticks) unsalted butter, softened	1 teaspoon vanilla

1. Heavily grease and flour a 10-inch tube pan.

2. In a large bowl or on a piece of waxed paper, combine 3 cups of the flour and the salt.

3. On a separate piece of waxed paper, combine the raisins with the remaining 2 tablespoons flour.

4. In a large bowl, cream together the butter and cream cheese. Gradually beat in the sugar. Beat in the eggs one at a time. Beat in the flour, then the vanilla. Stir in the raisins.

5. Spoon into the prepared pan. Place in a cold oven. Turn the heat to 325°F and bake for 1 hour and 30 minutes or until a wooden pick inserted into the center comes out clean.

Me and Shirley "Jean" Nesmith, with her famous pound cakes.

Luscious Lemony Pound Cake

Makes 12 servings

Sallie Brown

Here's another wonderful recipe from our neighbor in Hemingway and my son Kenneth's mother-in-law, Sallie Brown. Every year, Sallie bakes this tender cake for the holidays, especially for Christmas, an important time in her house. Sallie makes plenty of delicious food, including her famous baked glazed ham, a turkey with stuffing, collard greens, potato salad, macaroni and cheese, and at least three or four desserts, including banana pudding, blackberry dumplings, and this lemony cake. While this cake is served plain for Christmas dinner, you can also eat it with vanilla ice cream as a late-night snack.

3 cups cake flour
½ cup self-rising flour
3 ½ cups sugar
2 cups (4 sticks) butter, softened
9 large eggs
1 ⅓ cups sour cream
1 teaspoon lemon extract

1. Preheat the oven to 300°F. Heavily grease and flour a 10-inch tube pan.

2. In a mixing bowl or on a piece of waxed paper, stir together both of the flours. In a large bowl, cream the sugar and butter. Beat in the eggs. Add the flour alternately with the sour cream, starting and ending with the flour. Beat for 3 minutes. Beat in the lemon extract.

3. Spoon the batter into the prepared pan. Bake for 1 hour and 45 minutes or until a toothpick inserted into the center comes out clean. Turn onto a rack to cool.

Marbled Sour Cream Coffee Cake

Makes 16 servings

Doretha Brown-McFadden

Doretha Brown-McFadden got this recipe from her boss and friend at work (Doretha teaches elementary school) Rose Tomaselli, who in turn got it from her mother.

It's really a sensational cake. Whenever there was a special occasion at Doretha's school, like someone's birthday, Rose would bring in the cake and share it with everyone. Doretha would bring some of the leftovers home to her children, who grew up spoiled by Rose's wonderful baking. At Christmastime, Rose would send Doretha home with a tin of cookies, all different kinds of Italian specialties, including miniature cannoli, butter cookies, and nut cookies. Eventually, Doretha got Rose's recipe for this coffee cake and has been making it for her three children, James, Kevin, and Lavette, ever since.

FOR THE TOPPING

1 cup chopped walnuts

3/4 cup firmly packed dark brown sugar

1/4 cup (1/2 stick) melted unsalted butter

2 tablespoons all-purpose flour

1 teaspoon ground cinnamon

1 teaspoon vanilla extract

FOR THE BATTER

3 cups sifted all-purpose flour

2 teaspoons baking powder

1 teaspoon baking soda

1 teaspoon salt

1 1/2 cups sugar

3/4 cup (1 1/2 sticks) unsalted butter, softened

4 large eggs, separated

One 16-ounce container sour cream

2 teaspoons vanilla extract

1 packet pre-melted unsweetened chocolate

or 1/2 ounce unsweetened chocolate, melted

continued

1. Preheat the oven to 350°F. Heavily grease and flour a tube pan.

2. To make the topping, in a medium bowl, combine all of the topping ingredients; set aside.

3. To prepare the batter, in a large bowl or on a piece of waxed paper, combine the flour, baking powder, baking soda, and salt.

4. In a large bowl, cream the sugar with the butter. Beat in the egg yolks one at a time until well combined. Beat in the flour alternately with the sour cream. Beat in the vanilla.

5. In a separate bowl, using clean beaters, beat the egg whites until stiff but not dry. Fold into the batter.

6. Spoon 2 cups of the batter into a medium bowl. Stir in the melted chocolate; set aside.

7. Spoon 2 cups of the vanilla batter into the prepared pan. Top with the chocolate batter and swirl lightly. Sprinkle one-third of the nut topping over the batter. Top with the remaining batter, then sprinkle with the remaining two-thirds of the topping.

8. Bake for 50 to 60 minutes or until a wooden toothpick inserted into the center comes out clean. Turn onto a rack to cool.

Coconut Pineapple Cake | *Makes 8 to 12 servings*

Dorothy Greggs

My cousin Dorothy is known all over Hemingway for her outstanding coconut pineapple cake. Dorothy just loves to bake, and this cake is her most requested recipe. It is a favorite with our whole family and especially with Dorothy's mother, my aunt Sarah.

Dorothy makes this cake to give to Sarah whenever she is traveling by train or airplane. If a flight attendant came by to offer Sarah a cup of coffee or a snack, she would say "No, thank you." Then she would reach in her bag and take out a package of this cake. She always turned to the people sitting next to her and asked if they cared for a piece. Usually, they politely declined—until the aroma of that great cake reached them. After a while they changed their minds and said, "I think I will have a piece of that cake." By the end of the trip, Sarah would have made a new friend. So whenever she was flying, Dorothy always packed an extra piece of cake because she knew that someone else on the plane was going to want it.

When you make this cake, take care to drain the pineapple very well or it will make the cake layers soggy.

1 ½ cups sugar	**FOR THE FILLING AND FROSTING**
1 cup (2 sticks) unsalted butter, softened	Two 8-ounce cans crushed pineapple,
3 large eggs	juice packed
3 cups self-rising flour	1 pound confectioners' sugar
1 ¼ cups milk	¼ cup heavy cream
1 teaspoon vanilla extract	One 7-ounce package sweetened, shredded
	coconut

continued

1. Preheat the oven to 350°F. Heavily grease and flour two 9-inch round cake pans.

2. In a large bowl, cream the sugar with the butter. Beat in the eggs. Beat in the flour alternately with the milk, starting and ending with the flour. Beat in the vanilla. Spread into the prepared cake pans. Bake for 30 to 35 minutes or until a wooden pick inserted into the center of the cake comes out clean. Turn onto a rack to cool.

3. To prepare the filling and frosting, drain the pineapple well, reserving 2 tablespoons of the juice. In a large bowl, stir together the confectioners' sugar, heavy cream, and the reserved 2 tablespoons pineapple juice. Stir in the drained pineapple and coconut.

4. Cut each cooled cake layer in half to form 4 layers. Spread the frosting over three of the cake layers. Stack the cake.

Coconut Layer Cake | *Makes 8 to 12 servings or 2½ cups frosting*

Virginia G. Wilson

Coconut layer cake is one of my favorite cakes to bake and eat. My mother used to make it for holidays, Sunday dinner, and birthday parties, and I always looked forward to a moist, creamy slice.

The best part of any coconut layer cake is definitely the frosting, which is just so sweet and fluffy. This is my cousin Virginia's recipe and it is the best of its kind. You can use it to fill and frost any of the layer cakes in this book, but it would be especially delicious with the butter cake on page 251 from my cousin Dorothy's Coconut Pineapple Cake recipe.

---

2 or 4 Coconut Pineapple Cake layers (page 251)

One 15-ounce can evaporated milk

½ cup sugar

1 tablespoon cornstarch

2 cups sweetened, shredded coconut

2 teaspoons vanilla extract

1. Prepare the cake layers and let cool.

2. In a 1½-quart saucepan, stir together the evaporated milk, sugar, and cornstarch. Bring to a boil over medium heat, stirring constantly. Stir in the coconut and vanilla. Use to fill a 4-layer cake or fill and frost a 2-layer cake.

Rainbow Jelly Cake | *Makes 8 servings*

Alberta Thompson

Jelly cakes are an old concept in Hemingway, since most people had plenty of home-made jelly made from the fruit in their yards. Rainbow cakes are a newer thing. You can make a rainbow cake two ways: like this one, baked in layers and then stacked on top of each other with filling in between, or as a marble cake baked in a Bundt or tube pan. Either way, rainbow cakes are quite beautiful and always a favorite on holidays, at picnics, or at bridal and baby shower parties.

Although we usually used apple jelly when we made jelly cakes (since we had apple trees in our yard), you can use whatever kind you like. Our friend Alberta says you can also use preserves.

1 cup (2 sticks) unsalted butter, softened

1 cup sugar

5 large eggs

1 cup water

3 tablespoons vegetable oil

2 tablespoons sour cream

2 tablespoons buttermilk

One 18.25-ounce box yellow cake mix

1 cup self-rising flour

1 teaspoon red food coloring (optional)

1 teaspoon green food coloring (optional)

One 12-ounce jar jelly (any flavor—Alberta uses apple jelly)

1. Preheat the oven to 350°F. Grease and flour three 8-inch round cake pans.

2. In a large bowl, cream together the butter and sugar. Beat in the eggs, water, oil, sour cream, and buttermilk.

3. Add the cake mix and flour. Beat until well combined. Pour 2 cups of the batter into a medium bowl. Stir in the red food coloring and pour into one of the cake pans.

4. Pour 2 cups of the remaining batter into another baking pan. Stir the green food coloring into the batter remaining in the bowl. Pour into the remaining baking pan. Bake the three cake layers for 25 to 30 minutes or until a wooden toothpick inserted into the center of the cake comes out clean. Let cool in the pans or racks for 20 minutes. Turn the cake layers onto racks to cool completely.

5. Cut each cake layer in half to form six layers. Spread jelly on each layer, except the top. Stack the layers, alternating colors, to form a six-layer cake.

Van, me and Bedelia, and Kenneth, from our original calendar, 1963.

Fudge-Frosted Six-Layer Cake

Makes 8 to 12 servings

Virginia G. Wilson

Crizette used to love a chocolate-frosted layer cake for her birthday when she was small, and I don't think she's changed her mind now that she's all grown up. This spectacular cake has six buttery yellow layers spread with chocolate fudge. It was the kind of cake my mother would bake when she made a party for any of the children's birthdays when they were in South Carolina. She would invite all the children from the whole community over to the house and cook up a huge dinner with the birthday child's favorite food. Chicken perlow was a favorite for dinner, and a layer cake made the best dessert. And you know what—it still does.

FOR THE CAKE

3 cups cake flour

2 teaspoons baking powder

1 ½ cups (3 sticks) unsalted butter, softened

½ cup (1 stick) margarine

2 ½ cups sugar

6 large eggs

One 5-ounce can evaporated milk

2 teaspoons vanilla extract

FOR THE FROSTING (see Note)

2 cups sugar

12 regular marshmallows

½ cup (1 stick) unsalted butter

½ cup evaporated milk

Pinch of salt

6 ounces semisweet chocolate morsels

1. Preheat the oven to 375°F. Heavily grease and flour three 9-inch round baking pans.

2. To make the cake, on a piece of waxed paper or in a large bowl, combine the flour and baking powder.

3. In a large bowl, beat together the butter and margarine. Add the sugar and beat until light and fluffy. Beat in the eggs. Mix in the flour alternately with the evaporated milk. Beat in the vanilla.

4. Spread the batter evenly among the prepared baking pans. Bake for 30 minutes or until a wooden toothpick comes out clean when inserted into the center. Turn the cake layers onto racks to cool.

5. When the cakes are cool, slice each layer in half to form six round cake layers.

6. To prepare the frosting, combine the sugar, marshmallows, butter, evaporated milk, and salt in a 2-quart saucepan. Cook for about 5 minutes over medium heat, stirring constantly, until the mixture comes to a boil and the butter and marshmallows have melted. Boil for 3 minutes, stirring constantly. Remove from the heat and stir in the chocolate morsels until melted.

7. While still hot, spread about ½ to ¾ cup of the frosting on each of the five cake layers and stack.

NOTE: If you want to frost the outside of the cake, you may need a second batch of the frosting.

Red Velvet Cake | *Makes 8 servings*

Mary M. Brown

This cake is as deep a red as there ever was and it is something to see. The layers are flavored with chocolate and the frosting is made from cream cheese, a delicious and unusual combination. Most everything about this cake is unusual, and that's what makes it so much fun to serve. The recipe is from our friend Mary, and we thank her very much.

2 ¼ cups sifted cake flour

2 teaspoons cocoa powder

1 teaspoon baking soda

1 teaspoon baking powder

1 teaspoon salt

1 ½ cups sugar

½ cup (1 stick) unsalted butter, softened

2 large eggs

1 cup buttermilk

2 ounces red food coloring

1 teaspoon distilled white vinegar

1 teaspoon vanilla

FOR THE FROSTING

One 8-ounce package cream cheese, softened

½ cup (1 stick) unsalted butter or margarine, softened

One 1-pound box confectioners' sugar

1 teaspoon vanilla extract

1 cup chopped pecans

1. Preheat the oven to 350°F. Grease and flour two 9-inch round cake pans.

2. In a medium bowl or on a piece of waxed paper, sift the flour, cocoa, baking soda, baking powder, and salt together; set aside.

3. In a large bowl, cream the sugar with the butter. Beat in the eggs one at a time.

4. Alternately add the flour mixture with the buttermilk. Beat in the food coloring and vinegar, then add the vanilla. Spread the batter evenly in the pans. Bake for 20 to 30 minutes or until a wooden toothpick inserted into the center comes out clean. Turn out onto a rack to cool.

5. To prepare the frosting, in a large bowl, cream the cream cheese and butter. Beat in the confectioners' sugar until fluffy. Beat in the vanilla. Stir in the pecans. Use to fill and frost the cake.

Pineapple Nut Cake | *Makes 16 servings*

Shirley "Jean" Pressley Nesmith

Although all the children looked forward to Christmastime at my mother's house, it did take a lot of work to get ready. In order for her to get everything done by Christmas Day, my mother had to start her preparations as soon as Thanksgiving was over.

One job we all did together was shelling nuts for Mama's baking. We used to spend an entire week sitting around the kitchen table, hitting nuts with a regular old hammer, since we didn't have nutcrackers back then. At first we didn't mind, but after cracking buckets and buckets of nuts, our fingers got tired and sore.

Once the nuts were shelled and Mama started baking and letting us lick out the bowls, we forgot all about how much work it was. Since you can buy your nuts already shelled, baking sweet nut cakes like this one goes much faster. But the children will still appreciate it if you let them lick out the bowl.

3 cups self-rising flour

½ teaspoon ground pumpkin pie spice

¼ teaspoon ground cinnamon

1 ¾ cups sugar

½ cup (1 stick) unsalted butter or margarine, softened

4 large eggs

One 8-ounce can crushed pineapple, juice packed, undrained

1 cup mashed banana

1 cup chopped, peeled apples

1 cup raisins

1 cup sweetened, shredded coconut

1 cup chopped pecans

1. In a medium bowl or on a piece of waxed paper, sift the flour, pumpkin pie spice, and cinnamon together.

2. In a large bowl, cream the sugar with the butter. Beat in the eggs. Add the flour mixture and beat until combined. Add the pineapple with juice, banana, apples, raisins, coconut, and pecans. Beat until combined.

3. Spoon the mixture into a well-greased and floured 10-cup tube pan.

4. Place in a cold oven. Turn the oven to 325°F and bake for 1¼ hours or until a wooden toothpick inserted into the center of the cake comes out clean. Turn onto a rack to cool.

Chocolate Eclair Cake | *Makes 10 to 12 servings*

Dottie Powell

Dottie Powell is one of our friends down in Hemingway, and she offered us this fabulous and easy recipe.

"It's the kind of cake," Dottie told us during the cook-off, "that is so easy to make you can whip it up early on Sunday morning before church, even if you didn't think you had time to make a dessert. I make it all the time, and everybody loves it."

FOR THE CHOCOLATE FROSTING
½ cup (1 stick) unsalted butter or margarine
1 cup sugar
½ cup cocoa
¼ cup milk

FOR THE FILLING
3 cups milk
Two 3.4-ounce packages instant French vanilla pudding
One 8-ounce container Cool Whip

TO FINISH
20 to 24 graham crackers
(10 to 12 whole double crackers)

1. To prepare the frosting, melt the butter in a 1½-quart saucepan. Stir in the sugar, cocoa, and milk. Bring to a boil over medium-high heat. Boil for 1 minute, stirring constantly. Set aside.

2. To prepare the filling, in a large bowl, beat the milk and pudding mix until thickened. Stir in the Cool Whip and set aside.

3. Lay enough graham crackers side by side to cover the bottom of a 9 × 13-inch baking pan. Spread half of the filling over the crackers. Place as many of the remaining crackers as necessary to form another layer over the pudding. Top with the remaining pudding. Spread the frosting over the pudding. Chill for at least 4 hours, or overnight.

Strawberry Punch Bowl Cake

Makes 16 to 20 servings

The Reverend William S. James and Edith F. James

Jeremiah's Reverend James and his wife, Edith, shared this unusual recipe with me at the cook-off in South Carolina. It's made from a delicious combination of angel food cake, fruit, and whipped cream, then topped with strawberry glaze. The way you serve it is unique, too. All the ingredients are piled into a crystal or clear glass punch bowl so that you can see the different layers, then you spoon the cake onto plates. It's a real attention-grabber, and you can be sure there wasn't a crumb left when the cook-off was over.

2 cups confectioners' sugar

One 5-ounce can evaporated milk

One 16-ounce container sour cream

One 16-ounce container Cool Whip, thawed

1 large angel food cake (homemade or store-bought), torn into bite-sized pieces

One 20-ounce can crushed pineapple, drained

Two 1-pound packages frozen unsweetened strawberries, thawed

1 package strawberry glaze

1. In a large bowl, stir together the confectioners' sugar and evaporated milk. Add the sour cream and Cool Whip. Stir in the angel food cake and pineapple.

2. In another bowl, combine the strawberries with the glaze (prepared according to package directions, if using dried).

3. Spoon the cake mixture into the bottom of a glass punch bowl. Top with the strawberry mixture. Let stand overnight in the refrigerator to set.

Old-Fashioned Sugar Cookies

Makes 3 dozen 2½-inch cookies

Elizabeth Harper Martin

Kids love these cookies. When my children were little, I used to let them help make some of the shapes with the cookie cutters. It was a great rainy-day activity—it brought the family together and gave all of us something positive to do. It's a good idea to have a variety of cookie cutters on hand. Get some alphabet-shaped cutters and let the kids cut out their names. Then give them colored sugar for sprinkling on top. These cookies are wonderful for snacks, parties, Christmas, and other special occasions.

2 ⅔ cups sifted all-purpose flour

2 teaspoons baking powder

½ teaspoon salt

¼ cup shortening

¼ cup (½ stick) unsalted butter, softened

1 cup sugar, plus extra for sprinkling

2 large eggs

1 teaspoon vanilla extract

1 large egg white, lightly beaten

1. Preheat the oven to 400°F.

2. In a medium bowl or on a piece of waxed paper, sift the flour, baking powder, and salt together.

3. In a large bowl, cream the shortening with the butter. Beat in the sugar, then the eggs and vanilla. On low speed, beat in the flour until all the flour is incorporated into the butter. Using your hands, form the dough into a ball.

4. Roll out the dough between two pieces of waxed paper until ¼ inch thick. Using biscuit or cookie cutters, cut into the desired shapes. Brush the cookie tops with egg white and sprinkle generously with sugar. Place on baking sheets and bake for 8 to 10 minutes or until the bottoms of the cookies are browned. Remove to a rack to cool.

Thomas Cooper's Renowned Lemonade

Makes 16 to 20 servings

Thomas Lee Cooper

Our friend Thomas has been making his marvelous lemonade for Jeremiah Church functions ever since I can remember. In August, at the annual church picnic, is when we all drink gallons and gallons of the stuff. Thomas also agreed to make the lemonade at the cook-off, and it was a good thing he did. That lemonade really kept all of us going as we tasted our way through the delicious dishes that everyone brought.

In the old days, Thomas's father used to make the lemonade, mixing it up in a big old barrel, the biggest one he could, since no matter how much lemonade he made, it always seemed to get finished. He passed that recipe on to his son, and now Thomas makes it in a forty-gallon plastic bucket. The lemonade still tastes the same—tart, very sweet, and very good.

Herbert, me, Van, and Bedelia, with two of Van's children, Sierra (standing) *and DeVaughn* (in Van's arms), *after church in Hemingway, 1997.*

6 to 8 lemons

½ cup bottled lemon juice (like ReaLemon juice)

1 gallon water

1 ½ cups sugar

2 ½ pounds ice

1. Wash the lemons, then squeeze them by hand into a 2-gallon container (you should have 1 cup of lemon juice). Slice the squeezed lemons and reserve.

2. Add the bottled lemon juice, water, and sugar to the container. Stir until the sugar dissolves.

3. Just before serving, add the ice and reserved lemon slices.

Index

casseroles:
   broccoli, macaroni, and cheese, 205
   crawfish, 149–150
   lima bean, 197
Cheddar cheese:
   in broccoli, macaroni, and cheese
      casserole, 205
   in golden brown macaroni and cheese,
      206–207
   in Modestine's sausage and grits pie,
      122
cheese:
   casserole with broccoli, macaroni and,
      205
   in creamy ham and potato scallop,
      176–177
   golden brown macaroni and, 206–207
   hog's head, 131–132
   mozzarella, in Coute's eggplant
      Parmesan, 190–191
   see also Cheddar cheese; cream cheese;
      Parmesan cheese
cheesecake, Vernell Bishop's luscious, 242
chicken:
   the absolute best southern fried, 82–83
   barbecued, 77
   Bedelia's Dijon-grilled, 86
   Bedelia's special oven-fried, 85
   gizzards, tender stewed, 96
   "herbal," 90
   innards, in cornbread stuffing, 219
   livers, southern fried, 91
   Modestine's peachy, 84
   and rice perlow, 88–89
   roast, 78–79
   salad, Sylvia's, 174

   soup, 69
   Van's garlic, 80–81
chicken broth:
   in creamy ham and potato scallop,
      176–177
   in creamy zucchini soup, 71
   in Vanessa's tomato-red rice, 203
   in white bean and sausage stew,
      124–125
chili from the A&J, 103
chitlins, holiday, 126–127
chocolate:
   eclair cake, 260
   in fudge-frosted six-layer cake, 256–257
   in marbled sour cream coffee cake,
      249–250
   in red velvet cake, 258
chops:
   daughter-in-law Sylvia's barbecued
      pork, 114–115
   smothered pork, 117
cobbler, peach, 224
coconut:
   custard pie, southern-style, 238
   layer cake, 253
   in mama's sweet potato poon, 229
   pineapple cake, 251–252
   in pineapple nut cake, 259
   in southern bread pudding, 225
coffee cake, marbled sour cream, 249–250
coleslaw, Odessa Dorsey's, 168
collard greens:
   in Bedelia's soulful stuffed mushrooms,
      182
   Frances's old-fashioned, 188
   with smoked turkey, Sylvia's, 187

grits:

    rise and shine salmon and bacon with,
        156

    and sausage pie, Modestine's, 122

Ham:

    baked, supreme, 123

    hocks, in pinto beans and gravy, 179

    and potato scallop, creamy, 176–177

    Sallie Brown's beautiful glazed, 121

    in white bean and sausage stew,
        124–125

hash, fried rabbit, 138–139

"herbal chicken," 90

herb and garlic mashed potatoes, 175

Hill, Vanessa, recipes of, 94, 123, 203, 237

hog's head cheese, 131–132

honey:

    in baked ham supreme, 123

    -grilled yellow squash, Herbert's, 194

    lemon tilefish, Kenneth's, 152–153

hush puppies, 201

James, Reverend William S. and Edith F.,
    recipe of, 261

Jamison, Evelyn, recipe of, 128

jelly cake, rainbow, 254–255

Lane, Camellia Chinnes, recipe of, 103

lemon(y):

    honey tilefish, Kenneth's, 152–153

    juice, in sweet and sour baked fish, 151

    pound cake, luscious, 248

lemonade, Thomas Cooper's renowned,
    263

lima bean casserole, 197

livers, southern fried chicken, 91

Macaroni:

    in beef vegetable soup, 70

    casserole with broccoli, cheese and,
        205

    and cheese, golden brown, 206–207

    salad, 170

McCant, Sam, recipe of, 138–139

McFadden, Mattie, recipe of, 96

McGill, Janice, recipe of, 164

marinated:

    pork roast, 116

    spareribs, Nan's extra-special, 120

marshmallows:

    in candy yams soufflé, 180

    in fudge-frosted six-layer cake,
        256–257

Martin, Elizabeth Harper, recipe of, 262

meat loaf, Wednesday night special, 106

minute steak with gravy, Frances's,
    100–101

mozzarella cheese:

    in broccoli, macaroni, and cheese
        casserole, 205

    in Coute's eggplant Parmesan,
        190–191

muffins, blueberry, 216

mushrooms, Bedelia's soulful stuffed,
    182

mustard greens, in country-style mixed
    greens and turnips, 189

pork (*continued*)

Frances's fabulous spareribs, 118–119

hog's head cheese, 131–132

holiday chitlins, 126–127

marinated roast, 116

Modestine's sausage and grits pie, 122

Nan's extra-special marinated spareribs, 120

rinds, fried, in crackling cornbread, 218

Sallie Brown's beautiful glazed ham, 121

salt, in fried rabbit hash, 138–139

smothered chops, 117

white bean and sausage stew, 124–125

potato(es):

in beef vegetable soup, 70

and ham scallop, creamy, 176–177

herb and garlic mashed, 175

new, string beans with, 178

salad, Tina's famous, 169

in seriously spicy shrimp stew, 161

in southern-style beef stew, 102

sweet, golden fried apples and, 181

in tender pot roast, 99

potlikker, 199

pot roast, tender, 99

poultry, *see* chicken; turkey

pound cake:

banana, 243

luscious lemony, 248

raisin, 246–247

sour cream, 244–245

Powell, Dottie, recipe of, 260

preserved pears, spicy, 233

preserves:

apricot, in sweet and sour sassy turkey wings, 94–95

pie, pear, 232

Pressley, Bertha "Bert," recipes of, 147, 157, 233

Pressley, Julia, recipe of, 82

puddings:

bread, sweet potato, 220

creamy banana, 226–227

southern bread, 225

Puryear, Nan, recipe of, 120

Rabbit hash, fried, 138–139

raccoon, in Dolly's delicious 'coon, 140–141

raisin(s):

and apple sauce, crispy roast duck with, 143–144

in mama's sweet potato poon, 229

in Odessa Dorsey's coleslaw, 168

in pineapple nut cake, 259

pound cake, 246–247

in southern bread pudding, 225

in sweet and sour baked fish, 151

in sweet potato pudding bread, 220

relishes:

Ruby Love's pickled okra, 73

Venice's sliced cucumber pickles, 74

rice:

Bedelia's sassy, 202

beefy, with onions, 204

perlow and chicken, 88–89

and shrimp, Annette's quick, 160

Vanessa's tomato-red, 203

roast:

  marinated pork, 116

  tender pot, 99

Salads:

  Bedelia's Vidalia-dressed garden,
      173

  black-eyed pea, 171

  colorful corn, 172

  crab delight, 164

  macaroni, 170

  Odessa Dorsey's coleslaw, 168

  Sylvia's chicken, 174

  Tina's famous potato, 169

salmon:

  and bacon with grits, rise and shine,
      156

  cakes, 157

sauce, apple and raisin, crispy roast duck
    with, 143–144

sausage:

  in black bean and oxtail stew, 107

  and grits pie, Modestine's, 122

  in Vanessa's tomato-red rice, 203

  and white bean stew, 124–125

seafood:

  Annette's quick shrimp and rice, 160

  crab and corn boil, 162

  crab salad delight, 164

  crawfish casserole, 149–150

  seriously spicy shrimp stew, 161

  see also fish

sherry, in Nan's extra-special marinated
    spareribs, 120

short ribs, barbecued beef, 104–105

shrimp:

  and rice, Annette's quick, 160

  stew, seriously spicy, 161

side dishes:

  Bedelia's sassy rice, 202

  Bedelia's soulful stuffed mushrooms,
      182

  beefy rice with onions, 204

  broccoli, macaroni, and cheese
      casserole, 205

  butter beans and okra, 196

  candy yams soufflé, 180

  Cassandra's zucchini pie, 195

  country-style cabbage, 186

  country-style mixed greens and
      turnips, 189

  Coute's eggplant Parmesan, 190–191

  creamy ham and potato scallop,
      176–177

  Crizette's crispy corn fritters, 200

  Crizette's garlic fried okra, 184

  Frances's old-fashioned collard greens,
      188

  garlic and herb mashed potatoes, 175

  golden brown macaroni and cheese,
      206–207

  golden fried sweet potatoes and apples,
      181

  Herbert's honey-grilled yellow squash,
      194

  Herbert's "hot as you like it" fried corn,
      192

  hush puppies, 201

  lima bean casserole, 197

  old-fashioned corn dumplings, 199

  pinto beans and gravy, 179

trout, Kenneth's "it's worth the struggle" baked, 154–155

tuna croquettes, 159

turkey:

smoked, in butter beans and okra, 196

smoked, Sylvia's collard greens with, 187

Sylvia's special roasted, 92–93

wings, sweet and sour sassy, 94–95

turnips:

in beef vegetable soup, 70

and mixed greens, country-style, 189

Vegetable beef soup, 70

venison, Dolly's barbecued, 136–137

venison, mail-order source for, 137

Vidalia onion, in Bedelia's Vidalia-dressed garden salad, 173

Walnuts, in marbled sour cream coffee cake, 249–250

white bean and sausage stew, 124–125

Wilson, Mattie, recipe of, 206–207

Wilson, Virginia G., recipes of, 253, 256–257

Woodbury, Modestine, recipes of, 84, 122, 204

Woods, Bedelia, recipes of, 85, 86, 104–105, 173, 182

Woods, Evelyn, recipe of, 159

Woods, Herbert, recipes of, 156, 181, 192, 194

Woods, Kenneth, recipes of, 152–153, 154–155

Woods, Van and Brenda, recipe of, 80

Yams soufflé, candy, 180

see also sweet potato(es)

yellow squash, Herbert's honey-grilled, 194

Zucchini:

pie, Cassandra's, 195

soup, creamy, 71